For Advanced Learners

DYNAMIC DISCUSSION

Navigating through Various Topics !

Business, Finance and Economics
Life and Health
Society
Technology
Education
Environment

CARROT HOUSE

CARROT HOUSE
P.O.Box #2924, St. Marys, Ontario, Canada

Dynamic Discussion

First published December 2006
Reprinted April 2014

Acquisitions Editor : Carrot Language Research & Development

ISBN 978 - 89 - 6732 - 039-3

Printed and distributed in Korea
9F, 488, Gangnam St., Gangnam-gu, Seoul 06120, Korea

Curriculum Map

Course	Title	Level	Text Book
General Conversation	Pre Get Up to Speed 1~2	1	
	New Get Up to Speed 1	2	
	New Get Up to Speed 2	3	
	New Get Up to Speed 3	4	
	New Get Up to Speed 4	5	
	Daily Focused English 1	1–2	
	Daily Focused English 2	1–2	
Discussion	Active Discussion 1	4	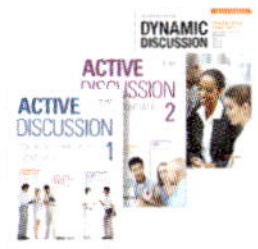
	Active Discussion 2	5	
	Dynamic Discussion	5–7	
	Chicken Soup Course	3–7	
	Dynamic Information & Digital Technology	4–7	
Business Conversation	Pre Business Basics 1	1–2	
	Pre Business Basics 2	1–3	
	Business Basics 1	2–4	
	Business Basics 2	3–5	
	Business Practice 1	4–6	
	Business Practice 2	5–7	
Global Biz Workshop	Effective Business Writing Skills (Workbook)	4–6	
	Effective Presentation Skills (Workbook)	4–6	
	Effective Negotiation Skills (Workbook)	5–7	
	Cross-Cultural Training 1~2 (Workbook)	5–7	
	Leadership Training Course (Workbook)	5–7	
Business Skills	Effective Business Writing Skills	4–5	
	Effective Meeting Skills	4–5	
	Business Communication (Negotiation)	4–5	
	Effective Presentation Skills	4–5	
	Marketing 1	5–6	
	Marketing 2	6–7	
	Management	6–7	
On the Job English	Human Resources	4–5	
	Accounting and Finance	4–5	
	Marketing and Sales	4–5	
	Production Management	4–5	
	Automotive	4–5	
	Banking and Commerce	4–5	
	Medical and Medicine	4–5	
	Information Technology	4–5	
	Construction	4–5	
	Construction English in Use 1~4	3–4	
	Public Service English in Use	3–4	

※ This Curriculum Map illustrates the entire line-up of textbooks at CARROT HOUSE.

Introduction

Carrot House Methodology

Andragogical Approach & Productive English

The teaching of children (pedagogy) and the teaching of adults (andragogy) are distinctively different. Pedagogy is akin to training and encourages convergent thinking and rote learning. It is compulsory, centered on the teacher and the imparting of information with minimal control by the learner. Andragogy, by contrast, is about education as freedom. It encourages divergent thinking and active learning. It is voluntary, learner-oriented and opens up vistas for continuous learning. Adults need to feel independent and in control of their learning. Therefore, Carrot House curriculum is based on andragogy and is designed to involve learners' participation and engagement by providing more task-based activities and opportunities to frequently interact in the classroom.

People want to achieve communicative competence when they learn other languages. English education in EFL environments has been rather focused on the receptive skills of English—listening and reading—which just increases learners' knowledge about language, not the competence of using it. If people are well-equipped with productive skills—speaking and writing—they will be competent in English communication. This is why Carrot House curriculum is designed to enhance learners' productive skills throughout the course. This andragogical approach of the Carrot House Curriculum, which focuses on productive English, will enable learners to achieve communication skills necessary for global competence. Carrot House's teaching philosophy and curriculum combined pursue a "Language for Success" for all learners.

Communicative Language Learning (CLL)

This communicative interaction, the essential component of language acquisition, does not occur in a typical, non-meaningful, fun-oriented conversation with native speakers. It occurs in a negotiated interaction through which a well-trained teacher provides comprehensible input that is appropriate to the learners. The learners actively utilize the opportunities given to them by the teachers.

To this end, the Communicative Language Learning (CLL) method is employed in the field of Foreign Language Acquisition. CLL provides activities that are geared toward using language pragmatically, authentically and functionally with the intention of achieving meaningful purposes.

Course Objectives

Dynamic Discussion is targeted at intermediate-high to advanced learners and it will generate both discussion and serious debate on a wide range of topics: **Business, Finance and Economics; Society; Life and Health; Technology; Education;** and **Environment.**

This book will allow students to assimilate methods to give logical and well-organized opinions with details on the selected topics. Students will enjoy presenting their ideas, while at the same time developing real confidence to debate.

Must-know Expressions

This section provides many useful expressions that students can use during their discussions. It is divided into several situations we generally encounter when we communicate.

Unit Composition

Each unit of this course book is divided into seven parts - Brainstorming, Reading, Core Message, Chunk and Chew, In-depth Discussion, Debating and Statistics.

■ Brainstorming

Learners are presented with one key word and a simple question related to the topic. Learners talk about the topic in small group and continue their conversation by brainstorming other key words and related questions.

■ Reading

This section covers a variety of controversial topics that provide learners with opportunities to debate by expressing their own thoughts and opinions.

■ Core Message

This section provides learners with an article to skim with the objective of catching the main idea or core message the writer is trying to deliver to the readers. This activity will help students check their understanding of the issues in the passage.

■ Chunk and Chew

The Core Message in each unit is followed by an exercise to reinforce the difficult or topic-specific chunks presented. Each unit has eight useful chunks together with two types of exercises: (1) to practice summarizing something they've learned by using chunks, and (2) to explain the meaning of a chunk in their own words or by providing synonyms.

■ In-depth Discussion

Learners share their opinions with a partner or other classmates by responding to the in-depth discussion questions.

■ Debating

Learners are provided with a statement which encourages them to debate by actively expressing their opinions. This section provides opportunities to learn how to organize their opinions and support their ideas. Moreover, learners can develop strategies of persuading others through the practice.

■ Statistics

This exercise provides a paragraph or an interesting story related to the topic. Learners are asked to create an effective title for the paragraph, which encourages them to summarize the main idea into a few words.

CARROT HOUSE

Category

Contents

Learning Icons

The icons listed below indicate the form of each activity.

Action Speech
Make a speech from the Power Position

Individual Work

Pair Work

Group Activities

Answer Key

Must-know Expressions for Discussion and Debating

Dynamic Discussion

Must-know Expressions for Discussion and Debating

Objective Business Expressions

• Beginning the Discussion

Let's talk about...

Let's discuss...

It's a good idea to begin with...

• Changing the Topic

The next point is...

Can we turn to [get to]...?

Let's move on [to]...

From now on, let's focus on...

Let's change the subject.

That's enough. It's time to change the subject.

• Proposing Another Meeting

Let's bring the matter up at the next meeting.

Let's discuss this issue on another occasion.

Let's come back to this point later.

Let's have another meeting on that matter.

• Asking Someone to Continue

Please go on.

Let's keep the conversation going.

Please go ahead.

So then?

• Referring to Material

Please take a look at... for reference.

Please consult...

You can refer to...

• Indicating Unfinished Business

It's not the best.

It's not settled yet.

We have to talk a little more.

It's not bad, but ...

• Objective Viewpoint

Objectively speaking, ...

If we take an objective view of..., ...

Please think of... objectively.

• Summary

To sum up...

In short, ...

To make a long story short, ...

Subjective Feelings, Opinions, and Judgments

• Expressing Feeling

I have a feeling that...

What's your feeling on...?

My feeling is that...

What's your impression of...?

• Subjective Viewpoint

Subjectively speaking, ...

The way I see it, ...

I think... is too subjective.

In my subjective view, ...

• Objection

I'm against....

I object to...

I'm opposed to...

I'm not in favor of...

I have a different opinion about it.

On the other hand, ...

My thinking is a bit different...

Could you clarify your point?

• Making Remarks

In my opinion [view]...

From my point of view, ...

As I see it, ...

• Judgment

In my own judgment, ... is right [wrong].

It's not reasonable to judge by appearance.

Judging from..., ...

I'll leave it to your judgment.

• Guess or Inference

I guess...

It's just a guess, but I infer...

I can reason that...

It seems to me that...

Comprehension, Questions, and Misunderstandings

• Resolving Misunderstandings

Do you mean to say...?

Did you really mean...?
I didn't quite mean it that way.
I'm sorry. I think you misunderstood what I meant.
Don't get me wrong.
Something seems to have gone wrong between us.
That's (quite) different from what I said.
That's not what I mean.

- **Understanding**

I see.
I see what you mean.
I see your point.
I understand what you mean.
I can catch [grasp] the point of what you're saying.
I can make sense of...
Yes, I know about...

- **When You Do Not Understand**

I don't know what you mean.
I'm not following you.
I don't get it.
I can't make out what he's saying.
What do you mean?
What does that mean?
Could you say that again, please?
It's beyond my understanding.
It's over my head.

- **Difficulty Understanding**

(It) is difficult to understand.
(It) is hard to make out.
Your question [answer] is vague.
I think your statement is ambiguous.

- **Lack of Explanation**

I think it needs further explanation.
That's not enough.
It's still beyond my understanding.
That doesn't make sense to me.

- **Clear Communication of Ideas**

What I'm really saying is that...
What I mean is that...

- **Asking for More Time**

Let's think about it.
How about giving it a little more thought?
Would you give me more time to think about it?

- **Repetition**

Excuse me?
Pardon (me)?
Would you say that again?
Would you repeat that, please?
I'm sorry, but I can't hear you.
Could you speak up, please?
I didn't catch what you said.
What did you say?
Say that again, please.

- **Grasping the Meaning or Point**

(Excuse me, but) what does... mean?
What do you mean by...?
What's your point?
I'm sorry, but I didn't get what you said.

Positive Comments and Remarks

- **Affirmation**

Sure.
Right.
Certainly.
Absolutely.
Exactly.
That's very good.
That's a good idea.
That's all right.
It sounds good [reasonable].
Thank you for giving an affirmative answer.
I think of... as positive.
What you're saying may be right.

- **Affirmative [Positive] Agreement**

You said it!
I think so.
You're right.
Of course.
I agree with you on that point.
I assent to your idea.
That is quite a good idea.
Oh, I agree entirely.
I am of the same opinion.
That's my idea, too.
That's exactly what I'm saying.

Must-know Expressions for Discussion and Debating

- **Partial Agreement**

I agree with part of what you said, but...
I agree with you to some extent, but...
Your point of view is all right, but...

- **Acceptance**

That sounds quite convincing to me.
You've made a good point.
You've convinced me.
I am convinced that...
It sounds right to...

Negative Comments and Remarks

- **Denial**

Certainly not.
Absolutely not.
Surely not.
Nothing at all.
Not at all.
Far from it.
Not really.
Not exactly.

- **Dissatisfaction**

I have something to complain about.
I have a complaint to make...
I'd like to complain about...

- **A Minor Matter**

It doesn't matter.
It isn't a matter of importance.
It's nothing.
It's a small thing.
It's not that important.

- **The Rejection of a Demand or a Proposal**

I'm afraid I can't accept...
That's absolutely unacceptable.
I'm afraid I can't...
It would be difficult to...

- **Exaggerated Explanation**

I'm afraid the story is a little exaggerated.
I think it's blown out of proportion.
That seems to be a bit of an exaggeration.

- **Disagreement**

I can't agree with you on that point.
I'm sorry, but I have a different opinion.
From my point of view, it's not reasonable.
I can't agree with you.
I don't think so.

- **Unreasonable Proposal**

It doesn't seem reasonable.
I don't think it's a good idea.

Politeness, Courtesy, and Requests

- **Appreciating Someone's Trouble**

I'm sorry to trouble you.
I appreciate your efforts.
Thank you for all your trouble.
You don't have to go to so much trouble.

- **Giving Another Opinion**

Besides, ...
In addition, ...
Added to this, ...
I have something to add to this.

- **Making an Additional Remark**

Could I add something?
There is one more thing to say.
Just one more thing.
I'd like to add...

- **Remarking on an Awkward Situation**

It's a little hard to say, but...
I don't know how to tell you this, but...
It's awkward to say, but...

- **Interruption**

I'm sorry to cut you off, but...
I'm sorry to interrupt, but...
Excuse me for interrupting, but...
Let's not discuss... any further.
Discussing [Talking about]... gets us nowhere.
Let's break off our discussion.
Discussing... further seems to be a waste of time.

- **Uncertain Answer**

That's a tough question for me.
I'm afraid I can't answer that right now.
I really don't have an answer.

I'll find out.
I don't know.

- **Request**

May I ask a favor of you?
Is it all right if...?
Would you mind [if I]...?

- **Asking for Help**

Would you help me?
I need your help.
I wonder if you could help me.

- **Apology (Regret)**

I'm sorry to...
It's a (great) pity that...
I am very disappointed about...
I regret...

- **Checking Another's Opinion**

Is that all right?
Can we discuss this?
Do you have any objection?
Would you agree?
Is that right?
Am I right?

- **Recognizing Errors**

I'm not sure, but I think (it) was a ridiculous mistake.
I apologize for my mistake.
It's my fault.
It'smy mistake alone.

- **Asking to Reconsider**

Why don't you think it over?
Please reconsider.
Could you think further about that?
Don't jump to conclusions.

- **Another Occasion**

Would you give me another chance?
Please let me try again.
Let's make it some other time.

- **Reservation of Answer**

I'm afraid I can't say yes at the moment.
I can't say anything now.
I'm sorry but I haven't decided yet.
I'll let you know later.
I have nothing further to say.

- **Consideration**

I'll think about...
Let me think about...
If possible...
I need some time to think about...

- **Taking a Memo**

Excuse me, but may I make a note of...?
Can I put down...?
Let me write down...
Just a minute. Let me get a pen.

Miscellaneous

- **Demand Choice**

Can you make a decision on this point?
The choice lies with you.
It's your choice.
Please do whatever you think is best.
It's up to you.

- **No Alternative**

I have no other choice.
There are no other ways of...

- **Decision or Conclusion**

That's already settled [fixed]...
Let's settle on...
That's the final decision.

- **Similar Instance or Expression**

In other words, ...
That is (to say), ...
..., so to speak, ...

- **Pointing Out Mistakes**

I'm afraid it was off topic.
I'm afraid your view is contrary to the popular sentiment.
I don't think you have it quite right.
It's unreasonable to say...
It's too much.
I think your statement is off the point.
Is it possible to get an answer on this?
Can you give me an answer?
Sorry... what are you trying to say?

Must-know Expressions for Discussion and Debating

• Unexpected Occurrence
You surprised me.
I hardly expected to...
I'm really surprised to hear... (that from you)
Really?

• No Connection
I have nothing to do with...
I have no connection with...
It's not your concern.

• Interest [Concern]
... be interested in...
... be very interesting.
... be of little interest.
Those things hold no interest for me.

• Soothing Mental Excitement
Please calm down.
Don't be upset.
Take it easy.
There's no need to get excited.

• Excuse
I have no excuse for...
What happened?
How did this happen?
Please don't make excuses.
I am not concerned with excuses... let's solve the problem.

• Joke
Just kidding!
This is no joking matter.
It is not something to joke about.
This is no time for jokes.
I meant it as a joke.
Please take it as a joke.

• Making Sarcastic Remarks
Don't make light of this.
This is serious.
Don't poke fun at...
I don't mean to be funny but...
It's not meant to be funny but...
Don't laugh but...

• Restraint
I think that's enough.
I think it's time to drop it.
Please, no more argument.
Could we please stop arguing this point?
I would appreciate if you would stop.
Can I make a point?
Please listen to what I have to say.
I would like to interject something.
Please, can we move on?
I think we've said enough on this.

• Rejecting Restraint
But this really is not of concern to you.
Sorry, but this is not your concern.
Please, I think I am doing fine without your input.
Wait! Let me finish (what I was saying).
Please let me finish.

• General Viewpoint
Generally (speaking), ...
On the whole, ...
Commonly, ...
As a (general) rule, ...

• Explaining the Situation
... be in trouble with...
... be in a position of...
... be at a disadvantage.

• Changing One's Position
Please put yourself in my shoes.
Just think what you would feel in my place.
If you were in my place, you would...

• Grasping the Intention
Please get straight to the point.
Let me know what's on your mind.
Let's be open with each other.
Please tell me what you really think.
Why? Please tell me what happened.

• Withdrawal of an Opinion
I'd better withdraw [take back] what I said.
I think you've said enough on the topic.
Your remarks are not helping at this point.
Could we consider another alternative (point of view)?

Discussion Topics

Dynamic Discussion

The Spirit of Giving

01

Brainstorming

Brainstorm keywords and ideas related to the topic and address the given question. Then, make a speech and share your opinion.

Charitable Donations

- **Generosity**

  It is better to give than receive. How can this be true?

-

-

Reading

The Charities Aid foundation recently used Gallup surveys conducted with 195,000 people in 153 countries worldwide to create the World Giving Index. The researchers **polled people about** altruistic acts they had completed in the previous month by asking questions about whether they had donated to charity, volunteered, or even helped a stranger. The results were promising and hinted at a large, helpful "global society." A fifth of those surveyed had volunteered, another third had donated money to charity, and around 45% of the world's population had acted as "Good Samaritans" by aiding a stranger.

The top donators were unsurprisingly wealthier nations, such as Australia and New Zealand, but close to half of the top twenty spots went to developing countries, including Guyana and Turkmenistan. Two of the world's largest countries **ranked at the bottom**—with India coming in at 134 and China at 147.

In some of the top countries, the practice of giving starts at a young age, with even kindergarteners being encouraged to bring in gifts or canned goods for charity at certain times of year. For these children, making donations can **naturally become a part of life.**

For countries that are not quite as generous, the wealthy should try to lead the way by making regular donations to groups that rely on contributions. The government could also **devise schemes** that will promote corporate as well as individual donations. At home, parents can **set an example** by selecting a charity or group for the family to support. When school children are **asked to contribute**, parents could talk about the benefits of donating and encourage their children to give from their own allowances.

Don't worry if you are cash poor! There are other ways to help out. You can still donate unwanted items to a needy cause, such as to aid **victims of natural disasters**. For example, you can drop off clothing to thrift shops or books to a school. These things might be useless to us, but could **prove quite valuable** to others.

Core Message

Talk about the core message of the article.

Chunk and Chew

Write the number of the meaningful chunk in the column next to its meaning. Then, by using each chunk, summarize something you have learned in the unit.

1 naturally become a part of life
2 to devise schemes
3 to poll people about
4 to prove quite valuable
5 to set an example
6 to ask to contribute
7 victims of natural disasters
8 to be ranked at the bottom

_____ to encourage a certain behavior by doing it yourself

_____ to ask questions of others to learn their opinions about a certain topic

_____ to demonstrate a large benefit to someone or something

_____ to become a lifestyle or habit of one's living

_____ to ask someone to make a donation of money or some type of item

_____ to be placed low on some sort of list ranking different things

_____ people who lose their homes or are otherwise affected by things like earthquakes or tsunamis

_____ to set up policies or incentives to encourage a certain behavior

1 _____

2 _____

3 _____

4 _____

5 _____

6 _____

7 _____

8 _____

Practice Discussing

1 What kind of mindset do people in your country have about donating?
2 What percentage of your salary are you willing to donate to charity?
3 Do you believe donating to charities is beneficial? Why or why not?
4 Have you ever donated anything to anyone or any organization? If so, what cause did you choose?
5 What policies does your government have for fostering the practice of giving? How else can they encourage people to contribute more to those in need?

Debating

Statement

Charity begins at home. The first priority of any family is financial security.

Do you agree or disagree with this statement? Why or why not? Please be specific.

Opinion :

Reason :

Support 1.

Support 2.

Support 3.

Summarize the opposing ideas.

Any rebuttal?

STATISTICS

0.6 meters

Create an effective title for the following paragraph.

Waitresses can increase their tips 22.6% by standing 0.6 meters closer to patrons (0.15 meters away versus 0.75 meters), according to Celine Jacob and Nicolas Gueguen of the University of Southern Brittany in France. The researchers say close proximity is one of four nonverbal ways for waitresses to boost tips, the others being smiling broadly, touching customers briefly on the arm or shoulder, and squatting next to the table when introducing themselves.

Fast Track to Globalization 02

Brainstorming

Brainstorm keywords and ideas related to the topic and address the given question. Then, make a speech and share your opinion.

Globalization

Business Innovation

Why is it necessary for companies to distinguish themselves from their competition?

Reading

Over the past few decades, the power balance of the world's economy has shifted. As new industries and technologies have **sprung forth**, previously unknown companies have **emerged as global powerhouses**. In light of this change, people the world over have become more accepting of diversity and outside influences. As many of the legal and cultural barriers that divided our nations in the past are broken down, people worldwide are **embracing the concept of globalization**.

Globalization is **the engine behind** the rapid technological development of the past century. As companies **fight to win their place** in the global marketplace, increased competition is forcing innovation. If a company fails **to think outside the box**, they run the risk of being left behind in the face of brutal domestic and foreign competition.

Innovation, however, isn't something that can **be conjured up** in government offices or corporate boardrooms. You can easily order people to work harder or modernize a factory, but it's just not possible to make someone think more creatively. That kind of change takes place inside the mind. This altered global market has made companies worldwide fiercer competitors. It is now essential to be open to outsiders and foreign ideas in order **to compete on a global scale.**

In today's world, knowing the needs of the domestic market is not enough. A successful company must also understand those of other countries. For that reason, companies must attain a wide-range of market-specific knowledge about countries that they interact with. This requires studying up on things like cultural norms and local laws, in addition to information about local customers' preferences.

As technology progresses, the world will undoubtedly continue to shrink as business continually transcend borders. For this reason, forward thinking is key to keeping up in our rapidly developing global economy.

Core Message

Talk about the core message of the article.

Chunk and Chew

Write the number of the meaningful chunk in the column next to its meaning. Then, by using each chunk, summarize something you have learned in the unit.

1 the engine behind
2 to spring forth
3 fight to win their place
4 be conjured up
5 to think outside the box
6 to embrace the concept of globalization
7 emerge as global powerhouses
8 to compete on a global scale

____ to be able to sell products around the world at competitive prices

____ to willingly accept the idea of a global marketplace and community

____ to think creatively or innovatively

____ to compete aggressively for a share of the market

____ to become a powerful or well-respected entity worldwid

____ to be brought to mind or imagined

____ the force responsible for

____ to rapidly come into existence or be created

1 ____
2 ____
3 ____
4 ____
5 ____
6 ____
7 ____
8 ____

Practice Discussing

1 Why do you think the ability to function in the global marketplace is critical for modern companies?
2 Do you think that global business practices and laws need to be standardized? Why or why not?
3 Why is it important for offices located in foreign countries to hire local people as managers and decision-makers?
4 What do you think are the reasons behind those distinguished domestic companies that could not expand globally?
5 In which industries does your country stand out globally? What are the reasons?

Debating

Statement

A company must have complete understanding of a local culture and marketplace to be successful when operating in a foreign country. For this reason, employing only local residents is essential to success.

Do you agree or disagree with this statement? Why or why not? Please be specific.

Opinion :

Reason :

Support 1.

Support 2.

Support 3.

Summarize the opposing ideas.

Any rebuttal?

STATISTICS

x3

Create an effective title for the following paragraph.

With the cost of diapering a baby running to approximately $1,500 per year, there are hints that American parents may be trying to save by skipping a few diaper changes, according to number-crunching by Advertising Age. The evidence: Disposable diaper sales fell 9% last year, three times the rate of decline in the number of babies age 2 and under, while sales of diaper-rash cream rose 2.8%. Babies get changed an average of 6.3 times a day in the U.S., according to Procter & Gamble, more often than babies in many other parts of the world, such as France (5.15) and Russia (3.84)

The Rise of the Childfree Family

03

Brainstorming

Brainstorm keywords and ideas related to the topic and address the given question. Then, make a speech and share your opinion.

Childfree

Social Policy

Should the government be offering incentives for people to have more children?

Reading

Birth rates across the European Union are **falling like a stone off a cliff.** Are these people childless or childfree? Once, women who once did not have children were called childless, with the very clear implication of some kind of loss. These days, an increasing number of women (as well as men) are strongly insisting on the term "childfree" with the main emphasis on freedom.

A rapidly increasing number of women in their 30s are very strongly rejecting the job for life description they believe is attached to parenting -loss of freedom, **reduced professional prospects,** and great financial burdens. There is no doubt that a rising number of people are actively choosing not to have children. The **mainstream media** is beginning to recognize the childfree lifestyle. People across Europe and the world are starting to feel they are not deviant for being different from the majority.

Despite such ideas, the idea of women actively choosing not to have children remains anathema to the majority of the people. Of note, it is also quite difficult for both men and women to obtain sterilization. In Europe, 2.1

children per woman are needed to maintain populations at their current levels.
The governments of France, Sweden, and Norway have good **pro-natal attitudes.** True or not, the governments of each of these countries believe that voluntary childlessness does not exist.

Marianna is a 30-year-old woman living in Linkoping, Sweden, and has met many fellow Swedes making the childfree choice. Marianna has known for some time that she never wanted to have children, and she is happy with her decision. Marianna says that in Sweden there exists much pressure from family and friends to have children. She hears the words "selfish and irresponsible" on almost a daily basis. She is becoming used to hearing these words, and they do not **register with her.** She notes an ever-increasing number of people in Sweden who are seriously questioning if children are really for them.

Jonathan McCalmont has founded Kidding Aside (The British Childfree Association) to fight for equality for people without children. Mr. McCalmont is disturbed at how the government is trying **to buy parental votes** with longer maternity pay, paternity leave, family tax breaks, and even flexible hours. He thinks the whole thing is **nothing more than a tax break** pretending to be a **social policy.**

He's also angry at what he thinks is money being transferred from those without children to those with children. There are childfree people who have serious responsibilities, such as looking after an aging parent. Mr. Mc Calmont thinks these people should receive equal benefits as parents do. "It is really up to individual people to decide what a family is," states Mr. Mc Calmont. "Why should the state make that decision?

Core Message

Talk about the core message of the article.

Chunk and Chew

Write the number of each meaningful chunk in the column next to its meaning. Then, using each chunk, summarize something you have learned in the unit.

1 fall like a stone off a cliff
2 reduced professional prospects
3 mainstream media
4 pro-natal attitudes.
5 to buy parental votes
6 register with her.
7 nothing more than a tax break
8 social policy.

societal or governmental attitudes or policies that favor couples having more children

to have limited job opportunities

the most viewed or listened to media in a country (TV, radio or newspaper)

to rapidly decrease

to offer government incentives to couples with children hoping that, in return ,the people will vote for the party in the next election

policies introduced by the government that have some social values

just to pay less taxes

to make somebody pay attention to something or realize/ acknowledge

1

2

3

4

5

6

7

8

Practice Discussing

1 How do you feel about the mainstream media portraying marriage as the time "when your fun is over"?
2 What is the long-term effect of fewer women having children?
3 Do you believe a smaller population just might be better for the world?
4 Are childfree people "selfish and irresponsible" or are they just honest in truly not wanting children?
5 How can government in your country support couples who want to have babies but can't?

Debating

Statement

It is imperative that the population of a country continues to grow every year to maintain a high standard of living.

Do you agree or disagree with this statement? Why or why not? Please be specific.

Opinion :

Reason :

Support 1.

Support 2.

Support 3.

Summarize the opposing ideas.

Any rebuttal?

STATISTICS

9%

Create an effective title for the following paragraph.

Postponing motherhood leads to an increase in women's earnings of 9% per year of delay, according to Amalia R. Miller of the University of Virginia. It also leads to an increase in wages of 3% and a rise in work hours of 6%, with the wage advantage being largest for college-educated women.

Frugal vs. Stingy

04

Brainstorming

Brainstorm keywords and ideas related to the topic and address the given question. Then, make a speech and share your opinion.

Savings

- **Miserly**
  - What are your spending habits?
  - Are you generous or stingy?

Reading

There is a big difference between the two: one is a **serious virtue** and the other is a serious shortcoming. Much depends upon how your perceived frugality impacts others.

One of my best friends here in Korea grew up on the poor side. He's no longer poor, but he almost always stays at the cheapest hotels when he is on vacation in Southeast Asia. Is he being **financially cautious**, or just plain stingy? What are the signals indicating frugality? What is the final crossover into outright Scrooge-like stinginess?

Naturally, many people believe that frugality or stinginess is **in the eye of the beholder.** Often times, a frugal person is just called stingy behind his or her back. Stinginess is often thought of as something that most people would not do. Perhaps such could be the case. There are really some key indicators that can be logically pointed out. Here are some general benchmarks: using 2-for-1 coupons at a restaurant might label you as frugal. However, you are clearly stingy if you base the food server's tip on the discounted final bill. Planning in advance what to spend on donating to charities is perfectly acceptable frugal behavior. If door-to-door charity solicitors throw rocks at your house, you're probably stingy.

Most of the time, frugality is a virtue. Such implies you are being careful, not foolish in the management of your financial resources. Stinginess is a mean and outright **anti-social vice.** Simply put, stinginess means a lack of generosity when the proper thing to do is to give.

Famous author and self-declared cheapo Mary Hunt **pulls no punches** when she gives her views on the Frugal vs. Stingy debate. The author of "Live Your Life at Half the Price," Mary believes that frugality allows her **to live below her means.** On the other hand, she says that stinginess requires other people to take part in your frugality. Stingy people **would not be caught dead** leaving a decent tip. They always split out meals and don't give a second thought to returning something worn only once. Such people never donate to their church nor do they thank their mail carrier with a small Christmas gift. In short, they do everything possible to keep as much money as they can. Stingy people make mistakes that are costly to all who come in contact with them. Of course, they often hurt themselves the most with their stinginess.

Always remember the golden rule. You don't have to give to everybody you meet, but spreading a little extra money around can bring a lot of good into your life. A spirit of generosity should give you a good feeling inside. **Looking within yourself** can give you the needed answer to decide whether or not you're being stingy.

Core Message

Talk about the core message of the article.

Chunk and Chew

The following sentences are from the article. Try to determine the meaning of each boldfaced phrase or chunk. Write a synonym or your own definition for each of the boldfaced phrases.

1 There is a big difference between the two: one is a **serious virtue** and the other is a serious shortcoming.

2 Is he just being **financially cautious,** or just plain stingy? What are the signals indicating frugality?

3 Naturally, many people believe that frugality or stinginess is **in the eye of the beholder.**

4 Stinginess is a mean and outright **anti-social vice.** Simply put, stinginess means a lack of generosity when the proper thing to do is to give.

5 Famous author and self-declared cheapo Mary Hunt **pulls no punches** when she gives her views on the Frugal vs. Stingy debate.

6 Mary believes that frugality allows her **to live below her means.**

7 Stingy people **would not be caught dead** leaving a decent tip.

8 **Looking within yourself** can give you the needed answer to decide whether or not you're being stingy.

In-depth Discussion Questions

1 Compare frugal behavior to stingy behavior.
2 What do you think makes a person stingy?
3 Have you known any stingy people? Give some examples of their stinginess.
4 Have you ever been accused of being stingy? How did you feel?
5 Do you agree that being generous in spending money can bring a lot of good into your life? If so, how?

Debating

Statement

People who live like misers all their lives and cannot part with their money often die rich but have a poor life.

Do you agree or disagree with this statement? Why or why not? Please be specific.

Opinion :

Reason :

Support 1.

Support 2.

Support 3.

Summarize the opposing ideas.

Any rebuttal?

STATISTICS

Create an effective title for the following paragraph.

2/3

Two-thirds of wealthy parents withhold at least some details about family assets from their children, and 15% disclose nothing at all, according to U.S. Trust's survey of about 450 Americans with $3 million or more of investable assets, excluding primary residences. The reasons include fears that the children will become lazy, squander money, or be taken advantage of. Additionally, 17% of parents in the survey believe their children won't be able to handle family money.

Computer Crackdowns On the Job

05

Brainstorming

Brainstorm keywords and ideas related to the topic and address the given question. Then, make a speech and share your opinion.

Internet

- Monitoring
  Is on-the-job internet monitoring common in your country?
-
-

Reading

Alicia Hewitt always knew the Washington Department of Labor and Industries had rules governing the use of computers during the working day. Ms. Hewitt thought this applied only to web surfing and not e-mail in general. She was **more than surprised** when she was fired after her office discovered 418 personal e-mails on her computer received over roughly a five-month period. This averaged about five messages per day.

Hewitt was an experienced eight-year agency veteran who always received fantastic employee performance reviews in addition to receiving certificates for outstanding customer service in her now-former position as a Workers' Compensation claims manager. Most of the seemingly innocent personal e-mails she received were messages about birthdays or lunch dates with co-workers. None of this meant anything when Hewitt's employer checked her entire office's e-mail after one of her co-workers **filed a** sexual harassment **complaint against** a supervisor in the department. Hewitt found herself one of the eight people fired from the department for improper use of department equipment.

Hewitt is not alone in **finding out** about office computer policy **the hard way.** Managers across the country are **cracking the whip** on employee Internet activity by **drawing up very strict rules and policies** and enforcing them with special software that monitors ALL web surfing, checks e-mail, and controls the types of sites an employee may go to. Vernon Wills, an employee at the Virginia Department of Business Assistance, **earned himself** a ten-day **unpaid suspension** for excessive Internet use on the job.

A survey conducted jointly by the American Management Association and the E-Policy Institute asked 526 businesses about their online policies and found that 76 percent record the sites their staff visit, and 65 percent block selected sites. In addition, some 55 percent review and retain employee e-mails, and 36 percent track all content on staff PC's, their keystrokes, and the total time spent on the keyboard. Lost productivity on the job due to web surfing is a serious concern and companies have many reasons to limit employee Internet access and activity.

Networks Unlimited is a Massachusetts-based Internet auditing company that specializes in auditing Internet surfing for their corporate clients. A monitoring box is installed on client companies' networks for a week, and then the company statistically **estimates longer-term usage** to figure out the number of hours per year employees surf online. In addition, the company also sells specialized technology to block and regulate employee Internet usage. According to the company, many executives **are shocked and surprised at** what their employees do while surfing online.

Core Message

Talk about the core message of the article.

Chunk and Chew

The following sentences are from the article. Try to determine the meaning of each boldfaced phrase or chunk. Write a synonym or your own definition for each of the boldfaced phrases.

1 She was **more than surprised** when she was fired after her office discovered 418 personal e-mails on her computer received over roughly a five-month period.

2 None of this meant anything when Hewitt's employer checked her entire office's e-mail after one of her co-workers **filed a** sexual harassment **complaint against** a supervisor in the department.

3 Hewitt is not alone in **finding out** about office computer policy **the hard way.**

4 Managers across the country are **cracking the whip** on employee Internet activity by drawing up very strict rules and policies.

5 Managers across the country are cracking the whip on employee Internet activity by **drawing up** very strict **rules and policies** and enforcing them with special software that monitors ALL web surfing, checks e-mail, and controls the types of sites an employee may go to.

6 Vernon Wills, an employee at the Virginia Department of Business Assistance, **earned himself a** ten-day **unpaid suspension** for excessive Internet use on the job.

7 According to the company, many executives **are shocked and surprised at** what their employees do while surfing online.

8 A monitoring box is installed on client companies' networks for a week and then the company statistically **estimates longer-term usage** to figure out the number of hours per year employees surf online.

In-depth Discussion Questions

1 Why are companies concerned with abuse of computer usage at work?

2 In your opinion, what is an appropriate punishment for employees who violate company regulations regarding personal use of company computers?

3 Is it appropriate for supervisors to monitor employees' computer use or is it an invasion of privacy?

4 Is there any difference between an employee using the company computer for personal use and using his/her own phone for personal use on company time?

5 Why is this issue of technology use now becoming so widespread?

Debating

Statement

Employees who abuse company policies should be immediately fired as an example to others.

Do you agree or disagree with this statement? Why or why not? Please be specific.

Opinion :

Reason :

Support 1.

Support 2.

Support 3.

Summarize the opposing ideas.

Any rebuttal?

STATISTICS

24/7

Create an effective title for the following paragraph.

In a survey by WorldatWork, 42% of employees in a range of industries said they believe that if their employer gives them a BlackBerry or other electronic device, it means they need to be available to the company all the time. Furthermore, 57% said they want clear boundaries between work and the rest of their lives.

Giving a Part of Yourself to Save a Life

06

Brainstorming

Brainstorm keywords and ideas related to the topic and address the given question. Then, make a speech and share your opinion.

The Gift of Life

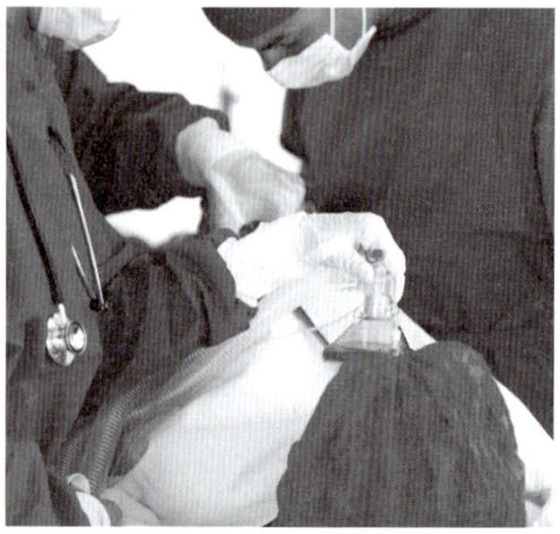

- **Transplants**

  Have you ever thought about giving your organs to save the lives of others?

-
-

Reading

The Ayala family had launched itself upon a sequence of nervy life-or-death adventures to arrive at the denouement last week. Anissa's leukemia was diagnosed three years ago. In such cases, the patient usually dies within five years unless she receives a marrow transplant. Abe and Mary Ayala began **a nationwide search for** a donor whose marrow would be a close match for Anissa's. The search, surrounded by much heart-rending publicity, failed.

The Ayalas did not **passively accept** their daughter's fate. They knew from their doctors that the best hope for Anissa lay in a marrow transplant form a sibling, but the marrow of her only brother, Airon, was incompatible. Her life, it seemed, could depend on a sibling who did not yet exist.

First, Abe had to have his vasectomy surgically reversed, a procedure with a success rate of just 40 percent.
That done, Mary Ayala ventured to become pregnant at the age of 43. The odds were one in four that the baby's bone marrow would match her sister's. In April 1998, Mary bore a daughter, Marissa. Fetal stem cells were extracted from the umbilical cord and frozen

for use along with the marrow in last week's transplant. Then everyone waited for the **optimum moment** - the baby had to grow old enough and strong enough to donate safely even while her older sister's time was waning.

Twelve days before the operation, Anissa began receiving intensive doses of radiation. Her immune system has gone out of business. But in two to four weeks, the new cells should take over and start their work of giving Anissa a new life.

The drama of the Ayalas - conceiving a baby, against such long odds, to save the older daughter, who would have died of chronic myelogenous leukemia - seemed to many to be a miracle. To some, it was **profoundly troubling**. What disturbed many was the spectacle of a baby being brought in to the world to serve as a means, **a biological resupply vehicle.** The baby did not consent to be used. The parents created the new life, then used that life for their own purposes, however worthy. Would the baby have agreed to the transplant if she had been able to make the choice?

The Ayalas' case resonated with meanings and dilemmas larger than itself. The case opened up a prospect of medical-technological possibilities and danger. In the past, it was mostly cadavers from which transplant organs were "harvested." Today, as with the Ayalas, life is being tapped to save life.

Most organs come from cadavers, but the number of living donors is rising. Last year, there were 1,773 who provided kidneys and 9 who provided portions of livers. Six of the living donors gave their hearts away. How? There were patient who needed heart-lung transplant packages. **To make way for** the new heart, they gave up the old one; doctors call it the "domino practice."

There will never be enough cadaver organs to fill the growing needs of people dying from organ or tissue failure. This places higher and higher importance, and risk, on living relatives who might serve as donors. Transplants become a matter of **high-stakes risk** calculations for the donor as well as the recipient, and the intense emotions involved sometimes have people **playing long shots.**

Core Message

Talk about the core message of the article.

Chunk and Chew

The following sentences are from the article. Try to determine the meaning of each boldfaced phrase or chunk. Write a synonym or your own definition for each of the boldfaced phrases.

1 Abe and Mary Ayala began a **nationwide search for** a donor whose marrow would be a close match for Anissa's.

2 The Ayalas did not **passively accept** their daughter's fate.

3 Then everyone waited for the **optimum moment** – the baby had to grow old enough and strong enough to donate safely even while her older sister's time was waning.

4 The drama of the Ayalas – conceiving a baby, against such long odds, to save the older daughter – seemed to many to be a miracle. To some, it was **profoundly troubling**.

5 What disturbed many was the spectacle of a baby being brought in to the world to serve as a means, **a biological resupply vehicle.**

6 **To make way for** the new heart, they gave up the old one; doctors call it the "domino practice."

7 Transplants become a matter of **high-stakes risk calculations** for the donor as well as the recipient, and the intense emotions involved sometimes have people playing long shots.

8 Transplants become a matter of high-stakes risk calculations for the donor as well as the recipient and the intense emotions involved sometimes have people **playing long shots.**

In-depth Discussion Questions

1 Would you do the same thing if you were in the Ayalas' shoes?
2 If your relative needed a kidney, would you donate one of yours?
3 Would you be willing to donate the organs of your deceased family member to other people in desperate need of them?
4 Do you think it's ethical for an organ donor to get compensation?
5 Organ transplants are still controversial, as there is sometimes great risk involved in the procedures or in the process of "harvesting" organs. Do you believe organ transplants are ethical and safe?

Debating

Statement

Using bone marrow from babies who cannot give their consent to such a medical procedure is unethical and should not be allowed.

Do you agree or disagree with this statement? Why or why not? Please be specific.

Opinion :

Reason :

Support 1.

Support 2.

Support 3.

Summarize the opposing ideas.

Any rebuttal?

STATISTICS

10 months

Create an effective title for the following paragraph.

Because of lower mortality from heart disease, a person who is born during an economic boom and survives to age 40 lives 10 months longer than an otherwise identical individual born during a recession, according to researchers led by Gerard J. van den Berg of the University of Mannheim in Germany. Their study of records on 6,000 Danes born from 1873 through 1906 shows that a mother's nutrition during the last months of pregnancy is crucial for her child's long-term cardiovascular health.

We're Really Not Cheapskates

07

Brainstorming

Brainstorm keywords and ideas related to the topic and address the given question. Then, make a speech and share your opinion.

Savings

- **Investments**

  What is the best way to invest your money? Why?

Reading

Does the thought of saving fully one-quarter of your income make you think of a **shoebox -sized** apartment? If so, say hello to Mitch and Lauren Marchand of Dallas, Texas.

Mitch works as a real estate lending specialist, and Lauren is a cost accountant. They have a common set of financial beliefs that allows them to spend with confidence - and **save industriously.** At the young ages of 28 and 27, Mitch and Lauren have accumulated well over $300,000 in assets. Both were certainly fortunate to get good jobs right after graduating from university. Their respective parents also paid for their college educations. Mitch and Lauren put their financial headstart to good use. The Marchands have **a combined household income** of $145,000 which includes annual bonuses totaling roughly $40,000. Of course, a good salary does not necessarily equal good savings. They have mortgage payments on a large 2,000 square foot (56 pyeong) home, and a serious love affair with luxurious imported cars. Just how do they save as much as they do?

"We have a philosophy: we can afford a lot more, but we prefer to pay ourselves first,"

Mitch says. "We want to decide whether we continue working at the age of 55, or to work part-time, or just travel whenever we want to. Nothing beats saving when you're young, so you can use the power of compounding to your advantage."

As you might expect, Mitch and Lauren set aside just slightly more than 25 percent of their income on a monthly basis. They also both contribute the maximum to their 401(k) plans at work and **take full advantage of** company matches. In addition, they have put the maximum possible into their Roth IRA's prior to hitting the income limits.

Aside from that, they really don't operate under an **ironclad budget** - more like strict values they regularly follow. They regularly **pay off credit cards in full** each month, so their only real debt is their home mortgage. Mitch says the large liquid cash holdings will be invested at some time in the future - he would really like to have an **emergency fund** comprised of 25 percent cash. He's presently talking to several investment advisors prior to investing his funds in the market. Mitch looks at negotiating prices as a very serious financial skill. He admits to never, ever **paying full sticker price** for a car.

What is coming in the future for the cost-conscious couple? The couple is more than ready to face their future burdens without giving up their saving ways. "We truly aren't cheapskates," Mitch says. "We really think over our financial decisions. We have a strong focus that moves us forward."

Core Message

Talk about the core message of the article.

Chunk and Chew

Write the number of each meaningful chunk in the column next to its meaning. Then, using each chunk, summarize something you have learned in the unit.

1 shoebox-sized	5 ironclad budget
2 to save industriously	6 to pay off credit cards in full
3 a combined household income	7 emergency fund
4 to take full advantage of something	8 pay full sticker price

_____ to save money diligently to have a regular savings plan

_____ very small, uncomfortable space

_____ to pay the price listed on the item price tag; to pay full price

_____ to maximize any opportunity that arises

_____ the total income of all working members living in the house

_____ a strict budget that allows for no deviation

_____ money set aside in case of an unexpected expenditure

_____ to not carry a balance forward month to month or incur interest charges

1 ______________________________

2 ______________________________

3 ______________________________

4 ______________________________

5 ______________________________

6 ______________________________

7 ______________________________

8 ______________________________

In-depth Discussion Questions

1. Do you believe the Marchands are too financially conservative?
2. Are you financially conservative? Why or why not?
3. When would you like to retire, and what would you want to do after that?
4. What percentage of your salary do you save?
5. Do you have a certain area in which you admit to a bit of overspending?

Debating

Statement

Investing in real estate is the safest way to guarantee a return on your investment.

Do you agree or disagree with this statement? Why or why not? Please be specific.

Opinion :

Reason :

Support 1.

Support 2.

Support 3.

Summarize the opposing ideas.

Any rebuttal?

STATISTICS

Create an effective title for the following paragraph.

55%

Despite improvement in the economy, 55% of U.S. employees saw significant declines in their savings in 2010, with older workers hit harder than their younger colleagues, according to a Towers Watson survey of 9,080 nongovernment workers. Older employees' uncertainty about their finances will delay retirements, posing workforce-planning challenges for companies, the firm says.

Penny Pinchers Gone Wild 08

Brainstorming

Brainstorm keywords and ideas related to the topic and address the given question. Then, make a speech and share your opinion.

Cutbacks

Corporate Cost Reductions

What is the most effective way of saving money in times of financial crisis?

Reading

There are idiotic and meaningless cost-cutting maneuvers by mega-corporations. We've hit that moment in every economic cycle, before the news gets unbelievably bad, when otherwise successful companies start grabbing their employees by the ankles, and **turn**ing them **upside down** in the vain hope that a few pennies and nickels might come tumbling out.

For example, the Financial Times has reported that behemoth investment bank Credit Suisse has told their bankers to reduce their color Xeroxing and **deal-making dinners** as part of an internal cost-reduction effort. The Wall Street Journal has reported that Yahoo! will require all U.S. employees to take either vacation or **unpaid time off** the week between Christmas and New Year's, as the company has become concerned about meeting targeted financial goals for the year.

These cost-reduction efforts are very different from the enormous cuts seen at crisis-laden companies like Ford. Yahoo! and Credit Suisse are attempting to prepare for an earnings slowdown as industrial conditions decline. Ford is **fight**ing **for its life** and so is offering to **"buy out"** unionized employees, slashing their white-collar workforce by a full one-third, and has even suspended its quarterly dividend. Ford's blunt cost-cutting knife, which takes something away from everybody ranging from assembly-line employees to shareholders, is damaging to morale. But this is accepted because the company is losing tons of money and everybody is sharing the weight of the burden.

On the other hand, cost-cutting at very profitable companies like Credit Suisse is imposed with a kind of ruthlessness you might see on "The Office." Since they're so arbitrary and meaningless, and because they're designed to bring maximum annoyance to all, they can be far more damaging to morale. What ends up aggravating employees is that the **Scrooge-like scrimping on** minor employee benefits exists right alongside a "pay whatever price for everything else" mentality. Credit Suisse has no problem paying **seven-figure bonuses** to hundreds of bankers each year. Then associates who prepare the deal books are told they can't print color slides with PowerPoint because the bank is watching.

Yahoo!'s cut-backs appear even more likely to anger. Right after a warning on revenues caused their stock to drop 10 percent, Yahoo! informed its 10,500 employees to take off the week between Christmas and New Year's. Offices will close, allowing employees to enjoy some guilt-free time while helping Yahoo! pare down unused vacation time. Taking into account an average of $2,000 per employee, such a bold move would save the company $21 million.

We will no doubt see plenty more examples of this type of corporate behavior as the economy continues to slow down and as increased interest rates **take their toll.** However, in the long run, saving a dollar now may well cost two or three dollars over time. Such so-called savings are not good for business.

Core Message

Talk about the core message of the article.

Chunk and Chew

Write the number of each meaningful chunk in the column next to its meaning. Then, using each chunk, summarize something you have learned in the unit.

1 turn upside down	5 buy out
2 deal-making dinners	6 Scrooge-like scrimping on
3 unpaid time off	7 seven-figure bonuses
4 to fight for its life	8 take one's toll

_____ a forced period of time off without pay

_____ to have a negative effect on someone; to cause damage or wear by hard living

_____ to do anything to try to stay in business

_____ to take over ownership of corporations and companies

_____ to invert something or someone; to change something completely

_____ dinners where potential clients are treated to lavish meals and abundant alcoholic beverages

_____ bonus payments in excess of $1 million

_____ to not spend any money like the Charles Dickens character, Ebenezer Scrooge

1
2
3
4
5
6
7
8

In-depth Discussion Questions

1 Discuss the pros and cons of cost-cutting in a declining economic environment.
2 Outline some possibilities resulting from the controversial budget cutting at Yahoo!.
3 If your company created a plan to exercise cost-cutting policies, what ideas would you recommend?
4 How would you react if your company told you to take unpaid time off from work?
5 Which company mentioned in the article would anger you the most if you were an employee there?

Debating

Statement

In times of financial crisis, companies must maintain their executive bonus programs to ensure that the company is being managed properly.

Do you agree or disagree with this statement? Why or why not? Please be specific.

Opinion :

Reason :

Support 1.

Support 2.

Support 3.

Summarize the opposing ideas.

Any rebuttal?

STATISTICS

40%

Create an effective title for the following paragraph.

Although nearly 40% of senior R&D managers say their companies are cutting back on research and development, a McKinsey survey finds that companies receiving the greatest benefit from R&D (strong growth, much of it from new products developed in house) are more likely to be increasing research budgets, expanding R&D activities, and shifting to longer-term, higher-risk projects. In other words, they see the downturn as an opportunity to upgrade their R&D capabilities and extend their competitive advantage.

Ocean Pollution

09

Brainstorming

Brainstorm keywords and ideas related to the topic and address the given question. Then, make a speech and share your opinion.

Pollution and Our Lives

- **Plastic Bags**
  - Do you use plastic bags for your grocery purchases?
  - What happens to those bags when you get home?

Reading

Plastic is literally **jamming up nature's code.** The very durability that makes plastic so useful to humans is exactly what makes it incredibly harmful to all the natural life cycles in every ecosystem around the world. When it comes to an accumulation of plastic in our oceans, David de Rothschild - expedition leader of the Plastiki, a boat made of 12,500 recycled plastic bottles - says the problem has **gotten out of control.**

For me, the stark reality of our planet's plastic situation really **kicked in** back in 2006 when I read the United Nations Environment Program publication, "Ecosystems and Biodiversity in Deep Waters and High Seas." The report pointed out that on or below every square mile of our ocean, there were 46,000 pieces of floating marine debris. The problem was particularly acute in certain areas.

The most notorious of these areas, called the Eastern Garbage Patch, is a swirling gyre in the North Pacific twice the size of Texas. There, for every pound of plankton, researchers found 6 pounds of plastic litter. Along with four other enormous gyres, these swirling heaps of trash now potentially cover up to 40 percent of our planet's surface. From ocean trenches in the Atlantic to floating particles across the farthest reaches of the Pacific, synthetic polymers **are on a rampage.**

As much as 90 to 95 percent of the total amount of marine debris is plastic- the remaining 5 to 10 percent is slowly degrading materials such as timber and glass, as well as hazardous and hard-to-clean-up medical, industrial, and raw-chemical sewage-related waste. The full effects of these man-made materials are still being fully assessed by the scientific community; however, it's safe to say that almost every fish, marine mammal, sea bird, and even human is or will be affected **in one way or another.**

But even more ominous is the second major issue regarding the spreading plastic plague: toxicity transference. In the open, ocean plastic photo-degrades, which means it absorbs the sun's photons and begins to break into simpler and simpler compounds without ever actually disappearing. Plastics also have a nasty affinity for oil; just think of the permanent ring left behind in a food container after storing spaghetti sauce.

The transference occurs as small amounts of these chemicals **work their way up the food chain**-from the filter feeders all the way up through to the fish sticks on a kitchen table. All over the world, children and adults are unwittingly exposing themselves to low levels of toxicity. Plastic is an odorless and tasteless parasite.

Now we must **shift our perception** of plastic from waste to a valuable resource. By refusing single-use throwaway plastics, we can slow-and in some cases even reverse-the alarming environmental damage occurring around the planet. Meeting this challenge doesn't even need to be a chore. It can be an adventure - the kind that gets you out of your car, office, or bed, and out into nature. There, you'll **understand viscerally** what it is that you're trying to save.

Core Message

Talk about the core message of the article.

Chunk and Chew

Write the number of each meaningful chunk in the column next to its meaning. Then, using each chunk, summarize something you have learned in the unit.

1 to jam up nature's code
2 to get out of control
3 to kick in
4 to be on a rampage
5 in one way or another
6 to work their way up the food chain
7 to shift one's perception
8 to understand viscerally

_____ somehow; using any method available
_____ a situation that is no longer controllable
_____ to spread something out of control
_____ to perceive instinctively or intuitively as opposed to intellectually
_____ to interfere with the natural sequence of events on the planet
_____ to change our thinking about something
_____ to start happening or operating
_____ small animals eat something toxic that is passed on to larger animals and eventually to humans

1
2
3
4
5
6
7
8

In-depth Discussion Questions

1 Do you believe that the problem in our oceans even exists, or is it the ramblings of a few alarmist environmentalists spreading a rumor?
2 If there is a major pollution problem in the oceans, why do you think this fact is not common knowledge?
3 Who is responsible for cleaning up the pollution in the oceans?
4 Why has plastic, in particular, become such a difficult environmental problem?
5 Do you agree that it is easy to ignore the pollution problem in the oceans because we cannot see it and it is therefore hard to imagine how big the problem is?

Debating

Statement

Pollution in the oceans will eventually kill all sea-life or, at the very least, make it impossible for humans to eat anything that comes from the sea, thereby destroying our oceans as a source of food.

Do you agree or disagree with this statement? Why or why not? Please be specific.

Opinion :

Reason :

Support 1.

Support 2.

Support 3.

Summarize the opposing ideas.

Any rebuttal?

STATISTICS

90%

Create an effective title for the following paragraph.

According to Francois Galgani of the French Institute for Exploration of the Sea, 90% of surface-water samples in the Mediterranean Sea yielded tiny pieces of plastic averaging 1.8 milligrams, many of them from discarded consumer goods. He estimates there are 250 billion such pieces of microdebris in the Mediterranean.

Changing Attitudes Create New Opportunities 10

Brainstorming

Brainstorm keywords and ideas related to the topic and address the given question. Then, make a speech and share your opinion.

Business Culture

- **Bias**

  Do you think changing attitudes in business will create new opportunities for young people?

Reading

Over the past hundred years, an unimaginable amount of social change has occurred. Societies and businesses alike have grown **more accepting of diversity**. This greater openness is **paving the way for** innovation and more opportunities for those who are willing to seize them.

Women's presence in the workforce is **truly a modern phenomenon**. Over time, higher educational institutions and workplaces have altered policies and long-held biases in order to guarantee sexual equality. This has led the female workforce participation rate **to rise to unprecedented highs** in many countries around the world.

In the past, it was all too common for women to encounter discrimination in the workplace. However, many of the old prejudices against women are **slowly melting away**. The trials of global competition are forcing many companies to value merit over gender. Now, companies strive to seek out unique thinkers and evaluate employees based on what they can **bring to the table** rather than their sex.

Other biases are also evaporating. Society has

become much more **accepting of alternative life choices**. Young people are veering away from the ideals of generations past, such as settling into a secure career and starting a family at a young age. This shift in priorities has encouraged many to take a leap and start their own companies, often in innovative fields.

Many of these young entrepreneurs are finding success doing what they love. Take the case of Mark Zuckerberg for instance. Thanks to a website he put together in his dorm- his net worth was estimated at a staggering $16.8 billion in 2013, making him easily one of the wealthiest self-made men of his generation. For many young people around the globe, this **new age of entrepreneurship and equality** represents something larger than a successful career—it represents a longing for more freedom.

Core Message

Talk about the core message of the article.

Chunk and Chew

The following sentences are from the article. Try to determine the meaning of each boldfaced phrase or chunk. Write a synonym or your own definition for each of the boldfaced phrases.

1 Societies and businesses alike have grown **more accepting of diversity**.

2 This greater openness is **paving the way for** innovation and more opportunities for those who are willing to seize them.

3 Women's presence in the workforce is **truly a modern phenomenon.**

4 This has led the female workforce participation rate **to rise to unprecedented highs** in many countries around the world.

5 However, many of the old prejudices against women are **slowly melting away**.

6 Now, companies strive to seek out unique thinkers and evaluate employees based on what they can **bring to the table** rather than their sex.

7 Society has become much more **accepting of alternative life choices.**

8 For many young people around the globe, this **new age of entrepreneurship and equality** represents something larger than a successful career—it represents a longing for more freedom.

Practice Discussing

1 As modern society is becoming more accepting of diversity, how will these new attitudes change business in the future?

2 How have women's roles changed in your country over the last century? Have any laws or policies contributed to this change?

3 In your opinion, will the influx of women in positions of responsibility have a positive or negative effect on business practices? Explain your answer.

4 What will be some of the positive benefits as more small businesses are created and start to thrive?

5 Could providing government assistance to new businesses be reverse discrimination against the established companies? Why or why not?

Debating

Statement

Women have to be better than their male counterparts to succeed in business.

Do you agree or disagree with this statement? Why or why not? Please be specific.

Opinion :

Reason :

Support 1.

Support 2.

Support 3.

Summarize the opposing ideas.

Any rebuttal?

STATISTICS

1/4

Create an effective title for the following paragraph.

CNN reports that 158,000 married fathers with children younger than 15 left the labor force for at least a year to care for their families while their wives went to work, according to a U.S. Census report based on data from last year. Dads are now the primary caregivers for about a quarter of the nation's 11.2 million preschoolers whose mothers work.

How About a Light?

11

Brainstorming

Brainstorm keywords and ideas related to the topic and address the given question. Then, make a speech and share your opinion.

Smoking

- Smokers in Korea

  What has been happening to the percentage of smokers around the world?

Reading

The time may not be quite right for senior tobacco executives to lean back in their padded chairs, pour some Scotch, and take a satisfied puff on one of their many profitable products. The certification of a class action lawsuit in the United States centering on "light" cigarettes threatens to cost tobacco companies untold hundreds of billions of dollars. If the industry is successful in stubbing out this case, it may well prove to be the last - in the United States, at least - of a wave of potentially crippling cases that has threatened the whole industry.

This current legal frontal charge on the big tobacco companies, commonly known as the Schwab Case, alleges that big name tobacco companies, including British American Tobacco, R.J Reynolds, and Philip Morris, **knowingly defrauded smokers** by selling what seemed to be healthier "light" cigarettes that were just as deadly as regular tobacco products. The tobacco industry could be forced to pay back the **incalculably large sum** of $200 billion in profits if they are convicted of this supposed deception. This amount could even be tripled under laws commonly used to combat organized crime.

Naturally, investors are clearly concerned, and tobacco shares fell after the recent announcement of the class action lawsuit. Losses were modest when one considers the large sums involved. This is due to the fact that investors have often discounted tobacco companies' value due to fears of legal action. It may also be because such companies have enjoyed **a long series of legal victories.**

The outcome of the United States Department of Justice's case against Big Tobacco just recently resulted in the shares of tobacco companies skyrocketing. The case, which started in 1999 and accused the tobacco firms of breaking numerous civil laws on racketeering, had originally aimed for some $280 billion of tobacco profits. The judge in the case ruled that tobacco companies had certainly been guilty of breaking the laws, but ordered that no monetary penalties should be paid after giving due consideration to a ruling in an unrelated case which concluded that such penalties were improper.

In direct contrast, the passion and resources of those taking on the tobacco titans may well dwindle. The chances that a case could fail or a court might reduce or strike down previously awarded sums appear to increase as the legal process **grinds forward.** Tobacco firms are remarkably skilled at **rebutting the claims** of those fighting on an individual level. Class action cases have their own **inherent weaknesses** as judges are reluctant to lump together the varying situations of many smokers into one case.

This is **by no means** an end to the dangers faced by Big Tobacco. While cigarette manufacturers face the most serious legal risks in America, litigation is either pending or ongoing in many other countries. Widespread smoking bans, public-health awareness programs, and various other measures are crimping demand in established markets. Restrictions are even starting to come in to the developing world, where tobacco firms have been most active in seeking new customers. The threat to the long-term **financial well-being** of tobacco companies could become much more serious if the governments of India and China ever turned against them.

Core Message

Talk about the core message of the article.

Chunk and Chew

The following sentences are from the article. Try to determine the meaning of each boldfaced phrase or chunk. Write a synonym or your own definition for each of the boldfaced phrases.

1. ... big name tobacco companies, including British American Tobacco, R.J Reynolds, and Philip Morris, **knowingly defrauded smokers** by selling what seemed to be healthier "light" cigarettes that were just as deadly as regular tobacco products.

2. The tobacco industry could be forced to pay back the **incalculably large sum** of $200 billion in profits if they are convicted of this supposed deception.

3. It may also be because such companies have enjoyed **a long series of legal victories**

4. The chances that a case could fail or a court might reduce or strike down previously awarded sums appear to increase as the legal process **grinds forward**.

5. Tobacco firms are remarkably skilled at **rebutting the claims** of those fighting on an individual level.

6. Class action cases have their own **inherent weaknesses** as judges are reluctant to lump together the varying situations of many smokers into one case.

7. This is **by no means** an end to the dangers faced by Big Tobacco.

8. The threat to the long-term **financial well-being** of tobacco companies could become much more serious if the governments of India and China ever turned against them.

In-depth Discussion Questions

1. Should tobacco companies be held legally liable for individuals who decide to smoke?
2. Discuss the level of the individual responsibility for deciding to smoke.
3. If a second-hand smoker wants to file a lawsuit, who should s/he sue: the first-hand smoker or the tobacco company?
4. How do you think employees from a tobacco company would feel about lawsuits against their company?
5. Do you agree that tobacco companies should be responsible for paying for a large percentage of health care costs because their products are responsible for so many health problems?

Debating

Statement

Smokers should pay more health tax than non-smokers since smoking is known to cause cancer and is a drain on the health care system.

Do you agree or disagree with this statement? Why or why not? Please be specific.

Opinion :

Reason :

Support 1.

Support 2.

Support 3.

Summarize the opposing ideas.

Any rebuttal?

STATISTICS

33%

Create an effective title for the following paragraph.

Tobacco use by Filipinos over the age of 15 dropped by 33% in households that bought a mobile phone, according to a World Bank study conducted by Julien Labonne and Robert S. Chase. When cash-strapped consumers in developing countries must choose among luxuries, many prefer the phone to the cigarette, the researchers say. Spending on mobile phones does not appear to have any tempering effect on alcohol consumption, however.

Men Also Suffer from Compulsive Shopping

12

Brainstorming

Brainstorm keywords and ideas related to the topic and address the given question. Then, make a speech and share your opinion.

Shopaholic

- **Compulsive**

  How would you describe yourself when it comes to shopping? Are you a compulsive shopper?

-

-

Reading

People like to buy nice or brand-new items whether they are men or women, but many women have been said to **be obsessed with** shopping. Actually, a lot of women admit that they **are addicted to shopping.** However, men are also beginning to confess that they are suffering from "compulsive shopping," too.

A recent survey found that 1 in 20 American adults buy things they may not want or will never need or use.
In today's world of consumerism, where we **are** constantly **bombarded by ads,** this is perhaps not surprising. What may **raise an eyebrow** or two is a further finding in the study that men are just as likely as women to suffer from "compulsive buying." Gone seem to be the days when women dragged their bored and fed-up-looking men around shopping malls.

The new research from Stanford University has revealed that men are now just as avid and compulsive shoppers as their female counterparts. Researcher Dr. Lorrin Koram said that the number of men who **indulge in unnecessary shopping sprees** has rocketed. "That's the biggest surprise – men engage in this behavior almost as commonly as women," he said. This finding **runs counter to** the conventional and rather stereotyped view that compulsive buying is very much a "woman's disease."

Dr. Koram said trends and figures may have been **unfairly skewed** as male obsessive shoppers used to be more reluctant than women to recognize that they had a problem and then come forward and admit it. He pointed out that, "Generally, in psychiatry, men seek care less often than women. It's not 'manly' to seek help." And help seems to be exactly what the doctor ordered for any compulsive shopper, who is usually not made any happier by his or her relentless buying. Dr. Koram warned, "It's always important to encourage people who have these types of disorders to seek treatment." Many find themselves **laden with debt** and filled with shame and suicidal tendencies as they attempt to hide their addiction.

In many societies, it's now becoming more and more difficult to discern the roles of men and women. This may be one of the reasons why there is an increasing number of men who also suffer from an endless impulse to go on unnecessary shopping sprees.

Core Message

Talk about the core message of the article.

Chunk and Chew

The following sentences are from the article. Try to determine the meaning of each boldfaced phrase or chunk. Write a synonym or your own definition for each of the boldfaced phrases.

1 People like to buy nice or brand-new items whether they are men or women, but many women have been said to **be obsessed with** shopping.

2 Actually, a lot of women admit that they **are addicted to shopping.**

3 In today's world of consumerism, where we **are** constantly **bombarded by ads**, this is perhaps not surprising.

4 What may **raise an eyebrow** or two is a further finding in the study that men are just as likely as women to suffer from "compulsive buying".

5 Researcher Dr. Lorrin Koram said that the number of men who **indulge in unnecessary shopping sprees** has rocketed.

6 This finding **runs counter to** the conventional and rather stereotyped view that compulsive buying is very much a "woman's disease."

7 Dr. Koram said trends and figures may have been **unfairly skewed** as male obsessive shoppers used to be more reluctant than women to recognize that they had a problem and then come forward and admit it.

8 Many find themselves **laden with debt** and filled with shame and suicidal tendencies as they attempt to hide their addiction.

In-depth Discussion Questions

1 What do you suppose makes men compulsive shoppers in today's world?

2 Have you ever regretted buying something? How can we fight the temptation to buy unnecessary items while shopping?

3 Do you think shopping boosts the economy, and vice versa?

4 What do you think of the people who buy luxury items? Do you think it's worth buying them or do you think buying them is a waste of money?

5 People obsessed with shopping need counseling. Retailers should help people by providing easy, unlimited return policies and access to professional help through well-advertised toll-free numbers. Do you agree? Qualify your answer.

Debating

Statement

There must be limits placed on advertising to prevent children and compulsive shoppers from being encouraged to buy products they do not need.

Do you agree or disagree with this statement? Why or why not? Please be specific.

Opinion :

Reason :

Support 1.

Support 2.

Support 3.

Summarize the opposing ideas.

Any rebuttal?

STATISTICS

26th

Create an effective title for the following paragraph.

People whose last names start with letters toward the end of the alphabet tend to respond more quickly to sales and other purchase opportunities, perhaps because they had to wait for things as schoolchildren, say Kurt A. Carlson of Georgetown University and Jacqueline M. Conard of Belmont University. Those with surnames beginning with early-alphabet letters tend to be slower to respond. The effect occurs only with childhood surnames, not names adopted because of marriage.

Honestly, I'm Not a Snob! 13

Brainstorming

Brainstorm keywords and ideas related to the topic and address the given question. Then, make a speech and share your opinion.

Classless Society

- **Ruling Class**
  - *Have you ever been in a situation where you felt out of place?*
-
-

Reading

Bill O'Reilly, the well-known Fox News talk show host, was in Washington for ex-President Bush's second term inauguration. He got an invitation to **a fancy dinner party. With a great deal of reluctance**, Bill accepted, but it really was not his kind of thing. O'Reilly holds to the belief that he is just a **low-level stiff among the elite** like many other people.

Bill had a very strange experience as a graduate student at Harvard's Kennedy School of Government (which was nice enough to allow Bill onto their sacred ground, he notes, "in an effort to bring different people together"). Other students' clothing was understated but of obviously top quality – and their rooms painted a picture of fancy vacations and **expansive family properties**. They did their best to try to be nice to Bill, but Bill was totally humiliated in a Thai restaurant because he didn't know how to order properly in Thai.

Many people are unaware of the fact that Thai is the special social language of the American White Anglo Saxon Protestant upper class. The explanation is indeed simple. American Jewish parents fresh off the boat often spoke Yiddish when they did not want others to understand what they were saying. White Anglo Saxon Protestants had only English. What could they do? Thus, Thai was adopted, which they use in the presence of the domestic help and the O'Reilly's of the world. At the age of 18, upper-class children attend a secret Thai school, craftily disguised as a ski resort, in Gstaad.

The very notion that the Kennedy School of Government reached out to the likes of O'Reilly, a poor orphan out of the pages of a Charles Dickens novel, as one on the bottom end of the human equation, would be truly amazing enough. O'Reilly's very first chapter on "The Class Factor" has some very puzzling contradictions. He introduces himself as "**Working class** Irish -American Bill O'Reilly quite far down on the social totem pole." He watched his father in the 1960's "**wearing himself out** commuting from Levittown" to work as an accountant at a large oil company. Bill also stated that Dad "never made more than $35,000"-which would equal $100,000 in today's dollars. Oh, the human tragedy! O'Reilly has been doing some downward social climbing. He is actually - and this is rather difficult to say in Thai -MIDDLE CLASS!

After all, why fake a humble and modest background? Well, business reasons do play a role: Joe Workingman versus the elitists is a good position for any talk show host, particularly one on Fox. Vanity is also another reason. It makes the climb to your current level more credible. There are also political reasons. Under our system, even conservatives need a believable theory to qualify for victim status, from which flows all blessings. The main reason is pure snobbery. And it is the only snobbery with real impact in America: reverse snobbery.

This is really not a bad thing. **Reverse snobbery** is a credit to democracy - it is egalitarianism going past the mark. In addition, it is a countervailing force against an increasing level of economic disparity. However, when you are faking it, if you are not careful, reverse snobbery has a way of looking like the real kind. Bill O'Reilly once said in an interview that he would never enter a Starbucks, due to the fact he prefers a Long lsland coffee shop "where fireman and construction workers hang out." Hey, Bill! Fireman and construction workers appreciate a good cup of coffee, too! They can also afford it. Starbucks is one of the greatest equalizing institutions of our day. Well, Bill, you would know that if you ever bothered going in there **every now and then**. No one likes a stuck-up snob, Bill.

Core Message

Talk about the core message of the article.

Chunk and Chew

Write the number of each meaningful chunk in the column next to its meaning. Then, using each chunk, summarize something you have learned in the unit.

1 a fancy dinner party
2 with a great deal of reluctance
3 low-level stiff among the elite
4 expansive family properties
5 working class
6 wear oneself out
7 reverse snobbery
8 every now and then

____ a dinner party that is very high class; often called a "black tie" affair

____ someone who travels in high society but doesn't really belong there

____ those people who work at laboring jobs, trades, or manual jobs where they work with their hands

____ large, rambling mansions located on many acres of land

____ to do something unwillingly

____ sometimes; not happening usually; every once in a while; occasionally

____ to work very hard; pushing oneself to work hard

____ poor or middle class people who mock or make fun of rich people

1 ____

2 ____

3 ____

4 ____

5 ____

6 ____

7 ____

8 ____

In-depth Discussion Questions

1 Discuss your thoughts and opinions on the role of class.
2 Is Bill O'Reilly a snob, a reverse snob, or is he just playing a particular role?
3 Is there an unseen class system that exists in Korean society?
4 Is prestige important to you? Why or why not?
5 Regardless of what country you examine in the world, it is the rich who rule. Is this statement true?
6 Is it possible that a country could operate in any other way or is the class system just the "way things are"?

Debating

Statement

Although America goes to great lengths to disguise the fact, it has a structured class system as strong as any other in the world. Money and power have created a very distinct ruling class in America.

Do you agree or disagree with this statement? Why or why not? Please be specific.

Opinion :

Reason :

Support 1.

Support 2.

Support 3.

Summarize the opposing ideas.

Any rebuttal?

STATISTICS

2.5 million

Create an effective title for the following paragraph.

In Russia, more than 2.5 million officials in politics, the police, taxation, education, and other fields receive a total of $40 million to $45 million per year in bribes, according to a paper by Yuriy Timofeyev of Volgograd State University.The results show that 21% of Russians admit to bribing tax inspectors, 16.2% to bribing police officers and judges, and 13.9% to bribing fire inspectors. The average Russian company pays $135,800 in bribes annually, the paper says.

Gaming Addiction

14

Brainstorming

Brainstorm keywords and ideas related to the topic and address the given question. Then, make a speech and share your opinion.

Computer Games

Addiction

Do you know anyone who is or has been addicted to computer gaming?

Reading

Video game addiction is a truly modern problem. Perhaps because it is so new, many people continue **to treat the disease lightly**. Although it may seem less problematic than other addictions, its effects can have **a devastating impact** on the social lives and careers of its sufferers.

The negative consequences of the **habitual overuse** of video games **manifest themselves in a variety of ways**. The addiction typically involves symptoms like withdrawal or anger when addicts are not able to play. It can result in addicts ignoring their own nutritional needs and can even lead to unimaginable situations, like the neglect of children. In a well-publicized case, a New Mexico woman was convicted of second degree murder and child abandonment after her three-and-a-half-year-old daughter died of malnutrition and dehydration while she was obsessively playing online games.

Users are **increasingly aware of** the addictive nature of the games and a few are even trying to fight back. In August 2010, a Hawaiian resident sued the game company NCSOFT for negligence for not warning that their products were so addictive. Claiming to have wasted 20,000 hours on one game over a 5-year period, he contended that he would have never started playing if he had **known there was a chance** that he could become addicted.

Despite the severity of gaming addiction, treatment centers are **not yet widespread;** however, this is gradually changing. The Chinese government has opened at least eight treatment clinics for compulsive gamers. In addition, the US opened a specialized rehabilitation center near Seattle. There is also help available online in the form of *Online Addicts Anonymous*, a US based non-profit organization that offers a 12-step program similar to *Alcoholics Anonymous*. As awareness of the problem spreads, addicts will be able to get the help that they need **to overcome their life-disrupting habit**.

Core Message

Talk about the core message of the article.

Chunk and Chew

Write the number of the meaningful chunk in the column next to its meaning. Then, by using each chunk, summarize something you have learned in the unit.

1 to treat the disease lightly	5 increasingly aware of
2 to know there was a chance	6 habitual overuse
3 not yet widespread	7 to overcome their life-disrupting habit
4 to manifest themselves in a variety of ways	8 a devastating impact

_____ using something excessively over a long period of time

_____ undesirable and difficult consequences

_____ to show up in many different forms

_____ not popular or widely available at the moment

_____ to be able to break a troubling habit or addiction

_____ to know that something could happen

_____ to not give the disease the respect or attention that it warrants

_____ noticing more and more

1

2

3

4

5

6

7

8

Practice Discussing

1 Why do you think many people today suffer from internet gaming addictions?
2 Do you think computer gaming addiction is a serious problem, or is it just sensationalized in the media?
3 Do you consider your smart phone a work tool or an entertainment device?
4 Could you survive without your computer or your smart phone? Elaborate on your answer.
5 What are some ways to prevent gaming addiction?

Debating

Statement

Regulating children's access to online games is not the responsibility of the government or other organizations. It is up to parents to monitor, educate, and discipline their children's behavior.

Do you agree or disagree with this statement? Why or why not? Please be specific.

Opinion :

Reason :

Support 1.

Support 2.

Support 3.

Summarize the opposing ideas.

Any rebuttal?

STATISTICS

62%

Create an effective title for the following paragraph.

Fully 62% of the web windows that college students open on their laptops during class are completely unrelated to the class, according to a study by James M. Kraushaar and David C. Novak, of the University of Vermont. Unsurprisingly, the students who allocate their cognitive resources this way get lower grades than their more attentive peers. Instant messaging is an "especially virulent" distraction, the researchers say.

Mobile Payments Are Coming

15

Brainstorming

Brainstorm keywords and ideas related to the topic and address the given question. Then, make a speech and share your opinion.

Life and Technology

- Mobile Apps

  Do you think technology is taking over our lives?

-

-

Reading

Tech companies and the financial industry promise us that smartphones will replace our wallets. Yet analysts say "**don't hold your breath**." Find out how these tools will make everything from shopping to commuting easier - and how long we'll have to wait for them.

The concept of waving your smartphone at a cash register to pay for groceries or a movie ticket has been talked about for years, but it's always seemed to be the flying car of retail transactions: awesome idea, but too logistically complicated to work outside of the sci-fi realm.

A recent announcement indicates that we may be **inching closer to this reality**. In May, Google announced a partnership with Citi and MasterCard to **begin road-testing** a mobile payment app called Google Wallet, beginning this year in New York and San Francisco.

"What's unique about 2010 and 2011 is that now we're **at a tipping point**," says Gwenn Bézard, research director at research and consulting firm Aite Group. "A lot of companies have made commitments and investments." On the other hand, there are issues of data security and ownership. Who's going to own all that valuable consumer data? Banks? Mobile carriers? Tech companies? These problems have kept mobile payments from really **picking up steam.**

The most noteworthy venture to date comes from Starbucks, which converts existing prepaid account cards into a digital format. Customers enter their Starbucks card number into a mobile app, which produces an image of the bar code that's on the back of their physical card. The cashier scans the phone barcode and the purchase amount is deducted from the account. This kind of software-based mobile payment is where analysts say we'll see the most activity at first, because it doesn't require merchants or the companies that manufacture card-swipe terminals to invest in new hardware.

So when will average Americans be able to **ditch their wallets** and whip out their phones at the cash register? And what sort of signs will we see **in the interim**? What you will see is a growing number of retailers experimenting with mobile tools and trying to get their customers used to tapping on their phones while in a store.

Analysts say most of us will still be stuck carting around both a phone and a wallet, but expect to see signs that the mobile payment revolution is under way in 2012. More retailers will embrace mobile and contactless technologies for non-payment tasks like inventory management. For instance, if the item you want isn't in stock at a big chain, you'll be able to see which nearby stores do have it and purchase it remotely on the spot.

Mobile wallets will tap into existing location-based loyalty and coupon programs to tell you **at the point of** sale if you're eligible for any discounts, coupons, or other promotions. Isis and Google Wallet are both working towards this end, but it'll take a few years to fill that wallet via buy-ins from merchants, carriers, and banks. At least marketers will have a few years to rethink the credit card slogan, "Don't leave home without it."

Core Message

Talk about the core message of the article.

Chunk and Chew

Write the number of each meaningful chunk in the column next to its meaning. Then, using each chunk, summarize something you have learned in the unit.

1 not hold your breath
2 to inch closer to
3 to begin road-testing
4 at a tipping point
5 to pick up steam
6 to ditch their wallets
7 in the interim
8 at the point of

____ in the mean time; in the period between the conclusion of one event and the commencement of another

____ to get rid of one's wallet as it will no longer be needed

____ do not stop breathing waiting for a situation or event to occur because it may take a long time

____ to do preliminary tests; trials

____ when a previously rare occurrence or situation becomes much more common;

____ to start to become much more effective or successful

____ to move slowly closer to achieving a goal

____ just before something is going to happen

1 ____

2 ____

3 ____

4 ____

5 ____

6 ____

7 ____

8 ____

In-depth Discussion Questions

1 Would you feel safe using your smartphone to make payments for purchases?
2 Is it really more convenient using a phone to make a payment than using a credit or debit card?
3 Do you think we have become too dependent on technology?
4 What are some of the benefits and drawbacks of using a smartphone?
5 In your opinion, what is the greatest value of using a smartphone?

Debating

Statement

The concept of phone payments is impossible not because of the complexity of the technology but because of the security risk of having a large concentration of personal and banking data available in one place.

Do you agree or disagree with this statement? Why or why not? Please be specific.

Opinion :

Reason :

Support 1.

Support 2.

Support 3.

Summarize the opposing ideas.

Any rebuttal?

STATISTICS

20%

Create an effective title for the following paragraph.

To understand credit card agreements, you typically need to be able to read at a 12th-grade level, but American adults read at just a 9th-grade level on average, according to an analysis by CreditCards.com. Only 20% of adults are capable of comprehending credit-card contracts, the site says.

The Relationship between Exams and Success in One's Life 16

Brainstorming

Brainstorm keywords and ideas related to the topic and address the given question. Then, make a speech and share your opinion.

Success

- **Study Hours**

  Do you think it is possible for a student to study 20 hours a day and be productive?

Reading

In countries around the world, students are preparing for exams that will supposedly **determine the course of their lives**. From a tender age, many children are prepped, schooled, coddled, and **groomed to get into** the best college possible and this often involves intensive preparation for college entrance exams. As many students and their families **shoot for acceptance into** so-called top-tier universities, students can feel crushed by the weight of these all-important tests and their perceived impact on their future success. But, what do these tests really measure?

It is a commonly held belief that standardized tests are **accurate indicators of** success and failure. Tests can determine what school we go to, the major that we are allowed to choose, and, in some professions, the ability to perform a given job. For this reason, the score has become the end goal of many schools. Our society has come to value teaching to the test more than **fostering intellectual growth**.

When you consider how many hours students devote to prep courses and practice exams, it is easy to appreciate why these tests are **not an accurate measure of** a student's academic potential. Instead, they are simply a measure of how well they can learn the format of a given test and information that is likely to appear.

For this reason, an increasing number of American universities, including the prestigious University of California, are debating making popular college entrance exams like the Scholastic Assessment Test (SAT) optional for their applicants. Research has shown that the correlation between SAT scores and first-year college grades is **minor at best** (only 10 to 20 percent of the variation in freshman grades can be attributed to the scores). By no longer requiring these scores, schools are freeing students **to broaden their interests** and avoid the dubious prep classes that past generations have been subjected to.

Core Message

Talk about the core message of the article.

Chunk and Chew

The following sentences are from the article. Try to determine the meaning of each boldfaced phrase or chunk. Write a synonym or your own definition for each of the boldfaced phrases.

1 In countries around the world, students are preparing for exams that will supposedly **determine the course of their lives.**

2 From a tender age, many children are prepped, schooled, coddled and **groomed to get into** the best college possible and this often involves intensive preparation for college entrance exams.

3 As many students and their families **shoot for acceptance into** so-called top-tier universities, students can feel crushed by the weight of these all-important tests and their perceived impact on their future success.

4 It is a commonly held belief that standardized tests are **accurate indicators of** success and failure.

5 Our society has come to value teaching to the test more than **fostering intellectual growth**.

6 When you consider how many hours students devote to prep courses and practice exams, it is easy to appreciate why these tests are **not an accurate measure of** a student's academic potential.

7 Research has shown that the correlation between SAT scores and first-year college grades is **minor at best** (only 10 to 20 percent of the variation in freshman grades can be attributed to the scores).

8 By no longer requiring these scores, schools are freeing students **to broaden their interests** and avoid the dubious prep classes that past generations have been subjected to.

Practice Discussing

1 Describe the education system of your country. Do you think that it values teaching for the tests or for intellectual growth? Why or why not?

2 Why do you think so much importance is placed on college entrance exams and school grades in today's society?

3 What factors are responsible for the stressful conditions that drive some students to contemplate suicide?

4 Do you think that emphasizing studying over everything else is a reasonable way to raise children? How do you plan to educate your own children?

5 What are some other good evaluation tools that can fairly represent students' overall performance in school?

Debating

Statement

Putting too much pressure on students can greatly impact their emotional stability and general health. For this reason, it is unreasonable to force students to take high-pressure tests.

Do you agree or disagree with this statement? Why or why not? Please be specific.

Opinion :

Reason :

Support 1.

Support 2.

Support 3.

Summarize the opposing ideas.

Any rebuttal?

STATISTICS

$36,000

Create an effective title for the following paragraph.

$36,000 was where Nick Enlow started the bidding when he put his 2008 Purdue University bachelor's degree in psychology up for auction on eBay, saying the diploma hadn't helped him get a job that paid enough to cover his $470 monthly student-loan repayment. eBay barred the auction, however, citing the "sensitivity" of the item, according to the Lafayette (Indiana) Journal & Courier.

Plastic Surgery for Employment

17

Brainstorming

Brainstorm keywords and ideas related to the topic and address the given question. Then, make a speech and share your opinion.

Plastic Surgery

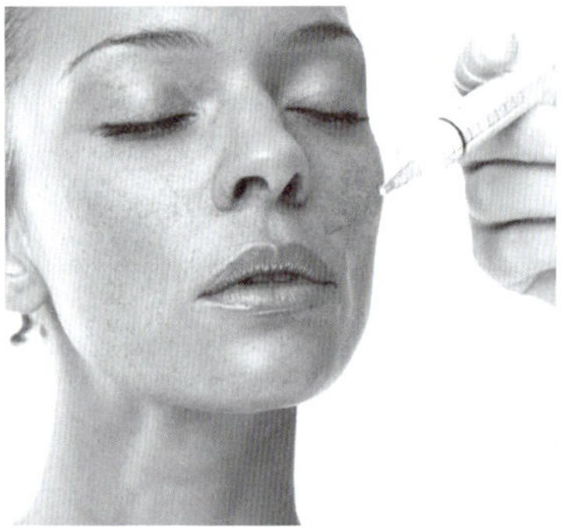

The New Resume

Would you have plastic surgery to enhance your chances of finding a job?

Reading

Once merely a means of improving one's appearance, plastic surgery is becoming an increasingly popular way for job seekers to **beef up their competitiveness**. Today's brutal job market is leading many people to go under the knife, in the hopes that improved features **will give them a leg up over** other interviewees.

A great deal of research has been conducted on the connection between beauty and success in the workplace. US economist Daniel Hamermesh's research demonstrates a so-called "plainness penalty"—with unattractive people earning up to 10 percent less than average looking people. In contrast, attractive people receive special treatment in the form of a "beauty premium"—which earns them approximately 5 percent more than their less fortunate counterparts.

According to the results of a survey conducted by a recruitment agency, 66.7 percent of those questioned concurred that a favorable appearance **is partly linked to** a good score in an interview. About 73.7 percent of respondents said they would favor a good looking/less skilled applicant over an unattractive/exceptional one.

"It is not appropriate to score applicants only **according to objective factors** such as academic scores or language certifications because a number of applicants have good grades and outstanding abilities. So, we are **giving more weight to** subjective criteria like first impressions and appearance," said one personnel officer.

With concern over **the declining economic situation** worldwide and so many new graduates flooding the job market each year, the high-paying jobs that most students are so eager to get just aren't available. As society continues to glamorize **little nips and tucks** and so many graduates continue to find the job market difficult, it is no wonder a growing number of job hunters are seeking an edge in looks. It's unclear whether improved looks or improved confidence and self-esteem resulting from plastic surgery are **the true key to success**, but one thing is certain: image matters.

Core Message

Talk about the core message of the article.

Chunk and Chew

The following sentences are from the article. Try to determine the meaning of each boldfaced phrase or chunk. Write a synonym or your own definition for each of the boldfaced phrases.

1 Once merely a means of improving one's appearance, plastic surgery is becoming an increasingly popular way for job seekers to **beef up their competitiveness.**

2 Today's brutal job market is leading many people to go under the knife, in the hopes that improved features **will give them a leg up over** other interviewees.

3 According to the results of a survey conducted by a recruitment agency, 66.7 percent of those questioned concurred that a favorable appearance **is partly linked to** a good score in an interview.

4 It is not appropriate to score applicants only **according to objective factors** such as academic scores or language certifications because a number of applicants have good grades and outstanding abilities.

5 So, we are **giving more weight to** subjective criteria like first impressions and appearance," said one personnel officer.

6 With concern over **the declining economic situation** worldwide and so many new graduates flooding the job market each year, the high-paying jobs that most students are so eager to get just aren't available.

7 As society continues to glamorize **little nips and tucks** and so many graduates continue to find the job market difficult, it is no wonder a growing number of job hunters are seeking an edge in looks.

8 It's unclear whether improved looks or improved confidence and self-esteem resulting from plastic surgery are **the true key to success**, but one thing is certain: image matters.

Practice Discussing

1 How popular is plastic surgery in your country? Do people feel the need to hide which surgeries they have had done from others? Are they embarrassed to talk about it?
2 If you had the opportunity to receive any plastic surgery procedure free, which body part would you choose to augment?
3 If one of your loved ones or close friends was unhappy with their appearance, would you encourage them to undergo plastic surgery?
4 How influential do you think one's appearance is for entering a company?
5 What factors are responsible for this emphasis on good looks?

Debating

Statement

Since most hiring officers are now making decisions based on appearance over ability, soon just about everyone seeking a job will need to have plastic surgery in order to compete in the job market.

Do you agree or disagree with this statement? Why or why not? Please be specific.

Opinion :

Reason :

Support 1.

Support 2.

Support 3.

Summarize the opposing ideas.

Any rebuttal?

STATISTICS

6%↓

Create an effective title for the following paragraph.

Starbucks customers in New York showed a 6% decrease in calories per transaction after restaurants were required to post calorie data, according to PhD candidate Bryan Bollinger and associate professors Phillip Leslie and Alan Sorensen of Stanford University. Most of the decrease comes from customers' buying fewer food items; nevertheless, Starbucks' overall revenue was unaffected by the new consumer behavior, the researchers report.

Micromarketing, Manipulative or Just Plain Smart?

18

Brainstorming

Brainstorm keywords and ideas related to the topic and address the given question. Then, make a speech and share your opinion.

Micromarketing

- **Demographics**

  How can differences among consumers affect their needs and purchasing habits?

Reading

What if there was a way to effectively **tap into the needs of** the individual consumer and to target people with ads and products that appeal to their personal needs? It seems like something out of a sci-fi flick, right? The future is closer than you think.

Micromarketing **has existed for ages**. Many companies and stores carefully monitor consumer purchasing habits to determine which products or advertisements will appeal to regional and even neighborhood demographics. **A prime example of this** is the American fast food giant McDonald's. The company boasts a wide range of products—many of them little known out of their specific regions.

Recent technological advances mean that advertising agencies can use information provided by consumers (or even stealthily collected from them) to help companies **get their message across to** their desired audience. Companies like Facebook **have got it down to an art**. The massive social-networking platform is now capable of utilizing not only user-provided data, but also information about users' online and offline purchases.

Collaborating with massive consumer data companies, like Acxiom, has given Facebook access to a score of data about members' "likes" both online and off. From this partnership, Facebook can ensure that advertisers **get the**

most bang for their buck by allowing them to narrow the parameters of their search to zero in on extremely specific markets. Suppose your ideal customer base is engaged, New York hamster-owners with an interest in racquetball—Facebook will hunt them down and show them your product.

Micromarketing seems like a win-win, both for companies **hawking their wares** and for consumers who are no longer subjected to viewing advertisements for irrelevant products, but there are some drawbacks. Due to the collection and analysis of personal data that give the ads their special touch, it remains a sensitive issue.

Core Message

Talk about the core message of the article.

Chunk and Chew

The following sentences are from the article. Try to determine the meaning of each boldfaced phrase or chunk. Write a synonym or your own definition for each of the boldfaced phrases.

1 What if there was a way to effectively **tap into the needs of** the individual consumer and to target people with ads and products that appeal to their personal needs?

2 Micromarketing **has existed for ages**.

3 **A prime example of this** is the American fast food giant McDonald's.

4 Recent technological advances mean that advertising agencies can use information provided by consumers (or even stealthily collected from them) to help companies **get their message across to** their desired audience.

5 Companies like Facebook **have got it down to an art**.

6 **Collaborating with** massive consumer data companies, like Acxiom, has given Facebook access to a score of data about members' "likes" both online and off.

7 From this partnership, Facebook can ensure that advertisers **get the most bang for their buck** by allowing them to narrow the parameters of their search to zero in on extremely specific markets.

8 Micromarketing seems like a win-win, both for companies **hawking their wares** and for consumers who are no longer subjected to viewing advertisements for irrelevant products, but there are some drawbacks.

Practice Discussing

1 What are some examples of micromarketing in your country?
2 How do you think advertising is able to affect our wants and needs?
3 Think of an example of an advertisement that really appealed to you. What was so special about the ad?
4 In contrast to micromarketing, macromarketing strategies target large groups of people indiscriminately. What are some cases where macromarketing strategies may be advantageous compared to micromarketing strategies?
5 What are the factors that are driving the micromarketing trend? Be specific.

Debating

Statement

Micromarketing strategies that involve the collection of consumer data are a violation of personal privacy. The government needs to enact policies to stop this unethical business practice.

Do you agree or disagree with this statement? Why or why not? Please be specific.

Opinion :

Reason :

Support 1.

Support 2.

Support 3.

Summarize the opposing ideas.

Any rebuttal?

STATISTICS

340

a day

Create an effective title for the following paragraph.

In China's Guandong province, one of the world's biggest manufacturing hubs, over 62,000 companies shut down in the last six months of 2008 – that's roughly 340 a day. With so many suppliers in dire straits, businesses have lost confidence in their vendors. According to a January 2009 HBR survey, 21% of 1,024 executives and managers said that their trust in suppliers had been shaken over the past 12 months.

Homelessness

19

Brainstorming

Brainstorm keywords and ideas related to the topic and address the given question. Then, make a speech and share your opinion.

Homelessness

Beggar

Are there many beggars in your country? Do you ever give money to beggars? Why or why not?

Reading

Homelessness is an issue that every country must deal with. It has no racial or national boundaries. Statistics for homelessness are more staggering than people know. Over 700,000 people are homeless on any given night in the richest country in the world, the United States.

The most common reason for homelessness in poorer, undeveloped countries is poverty. In advanced countries, this is usually not the case for homelessness. Many misunderstandings arise on the part of the public when it comes to the subject of homelessness, especially in richer countries. The misconception that the homeless are lazy and do not want to work is not true. Many homeless people have jobs, but they do not make enough money to pay for both shelter and sustenance. Food always **wins out** in the choice between housing and eating. A big problem is the housing prices. Most homeless people live in large cities where the rent is higher and living expenses are costly.

There are many other reasons behind homelessness such as domestic violence, dissatisfaction with home life, and racism. Women who are abused by their husbands try to escape to places where they can't be found and usually **end up on the streets**. It may be harder for members of a certain race to find work in some rich countries, so they are forced to live on the streets. Some teenagers run away from home because they do not want to live under the control of their parents.

A welfare system helps people who are homeless **for one reason or another**. Most countries have these programs set up for homeless people. Places such as **soup kitchens**, and homeless shelters along with food stamp programs are provided by the government. They also issue monthly welfare checks to needy people. Many American citizens argue that the U.S. welfare system is too generous and makes recipients of these monthly checks lazy. Some think that it takes away their incentive to work. The welfare systems in European countries are even more generous. These systems are beginning to **become a drag on their economies**. Europeans countries who spent an average of 51 percent on welfare systems are feeling the effects in their economy.

In Asia, however, welfare systems **lag far behind** those previously mentioned. Except for Japan, Asian countries receive money to help the needy from private sources, not the government. More **affluent countries** like South Korea and Taiwan are quickly developing these programs. The countries provide **universal health care coverage** for all of their citizens.

Core Message

Talk about the core message of the article.

Chunk and Chew

Write the number of each meaningful chunk in the column next to its meaning. Then, using each chunk, summarize something you have learned in the unit.

1 to win out
2 end up on the streets
3 for one reason or another
4 soup kitchens
5 to become a drag on one's economy
6 to lag far behind
7 affluent countries
8 universal health care coverage

_____ government-sponsored healthcare available at little or no cost

_____ countries where people enjoy a high standard of living with good family incomes

_____ to slow down or hinder the development or progress of the economy

_____ to succeed or to be chosen over other options; to finish first after great effort

_____ to fail to keep up the pace; to develop slowly

_____ a place usually set up by a charitable organization to give free meals to homeless people

_____ for a number of possible reasons; taking many options into consideration

_____ to have no choice but to live on the streets

1 _____

2 _____

3 _____

4 _____

5 _____

6 _____

7 _____

8 _____

In-depth Discussion Questions

1 Are there many homeless people in your country? If so, where can they be seen?

2 Where do most of the homeless people in your country sleep at night? Are they allowed to sleep in the parks or other public places?

3 Do you think the welfare programs in your country are sufficient to take care of all the poor and homeless people? If not, what more should the government do?

4 Countries in Europe are now spending over half of their GDP on welfare programs for the homeless and poor. It is hurting their economies. What should these countries do?

5 Contrary to popular belief, homelessness is not always a result of poverty. What circumstances can result in people living in the streets?

Debating

Statement

Most homeless people live on the streets by choice, so it is a waste of resources to try to help them.

Do you agree or disagree with this statement? Why or why not? Please be specific.

Opinion :

Reason :

Support 1.

Support 2.

Support 3.

Summarize the opposing ideas.

Any rebuttal?

STATISTICS

<1%

Create an effective title for the following paragraph.

The advanced "clean" technology sector is so small that it accounts for less than 1% of U.S. nonfarm employment and thus is probably incapable of creating large numbers of jobs, according to McKinsey. Low-tech green work such as replacing old heating equipment could be a better job generator; in fact, service sectors were responsible for the vast majority of new employment from 1995 to 2005, producing 100% of net jobs in rich countries and 85% in emerging economies.

Cross-Border Pollution

20

Brainstorming

Brainstorm keywords and ideas related to the topic and address the given question. Then, make a speech and share your opinion.

Pollution

Cross-Border Pollution Effects

What are some effects of cross-border pollution that you are aware of?

Reading

It's a natural fact that wind and water don't respect national boundaries. One country's pollution quickly can, and often does, become another country's environmental and economic crisis. And because the problem originates in another country, solving it becomes a matter of diplomacy and international relations, leaving the local people who are most affected with few real options.

A good example of this phenomenon is occurring in Asia, where cross-border pollution from China is causing serious environmental problems in Japan and South Korea as the Chinese continue to expand their economy **at great environmental cost.**

Schools in southern Japan and South Korea have had to suspend classes or restrict activities because of toxic chemical smog from China's factories or sand storms from the Gobi Desert, which are either caused or made worse by severe deforestation. And in late 2005, an explosion at a chemical plant in northeastern China spilled benzene into the Songhua River, contaminating the drinking water of Russian cities downstream from the spill. The environmental ministers of China, Japan and

South Korea agreed to look at the problem together a few years ago. The goal is for Asian nations to develop a treaty on cross-border air pollution similar to agreements among nations in Europe and North America, but progress is slow and the inevitable **political finger-pointing** slows it even more.

China is not alone as it struggles to find a **workable balance between** economic growth **and** environmental sustainability. Japan also created severe air and water pollution as it pushed hard to become the world's second largest economy after World War II. Thankfully, the situation has improved since the 1970s when environmental regulations were imposed.

China has taken several steps recently to lessen its environmental impact, including announcing a plan to invest $175 billion (¥1.4 trillion) in environmental protection for about 4 years. China also **made a commitment** to **phase out** incandescent light bulbs in favor of more energy-efficient compact fluorescent bulbs— a move that could reduce global greenhouse gas emissions by 500 million tons annually. And China pledged to ban the production, sale, and use of thin plastic bags within six months.

China is also taking part in international talks aimed at negotiating a new treaty on greenhouse gas emissions and global warming, which will replace the Kyoto Protocol when it expires. Before long, China is expected to surpass the United States as the nation most responsible for greenhouse gas emissions worldwide— a cross-border pollution **problem of global proportions**.

Despite these efforts, environmental degradation in China and other developing countries in Asia—including the problem of cross-border pollution—**is likely to get worse before it gets better**. According to an environmental study, emissions of nitrogen oxide-a greenhouse gas that is the primary cause of urban smog-are expected to increase 2.3 times in China and 1.4 times in East Asia by 2020 if China and other nations do nothing to curb them. **A lack of political leadership** in East Asia would mean a worldwide worsening of air quality.

Core Message

Talk about the core message of the article.

Chunk and Chew

Write the number of each meaningful chunk in the column next to its meaning. Then, using each chunk, summarize something you have learned in the unit.

1 at great environmental cost
2 political finger-pointing
3 workable balance between A and B
4 to make a commitment
5 to phase out
6 problem of global proportions
7 be likely to get worse before it gets better
8 a lack of political leadership

____ (a situation) will not improve soon and will worsen
____ political leaders are unwilling to take a strong stance on environmental issues
____ a problem that affects the entire planet
____ to continue something without concern for the impact on the environment
____ each government blaming the other for the problem
____ an effective or practical solution; capability of being handled through balance
____ to slowly remove from production; to bring to an end, one stage at a time
____ to make a pledge or a promise to complete a specific action

1
2
3
4
5
6
7
8

Practice Discussing

1 What are some ways to prevent cross-border pollution?
2 China is continuously becoming a greater industrialized nation with greater economic power. Do you think it will be easier or harder to convince them to cut back their cross-border pollution issues?
3 Do you think your own country is doing a good job at reducing pollution so it does not affect your neighbors?
4 What are some good ways to minimize pollution?
5 *"A lack of political leadership in East Asia would mean a worldwid worsening of air quality."* This state ment was made by the head of air pollution monitoring research at Japan's National Institute for Environmental Study. What do you think?

Debating

Statement

Pollution generated in one country and migrating to another is the sole responsibility of the country of origin. The country of origin must be accountable for clean up and any other costs. Enforcing such a rule is the only way to contain cross-border pollution.

Do you agree or disagree with this statement? Why or why not? Please be specific.

Opinion :

Reason :

Support 1.

Support 2.

Support 3.

Summarize the opposing ideas.

Any rebuttal?

STATISTICS

8.4 gigatons

Create an effective title for the following paragraph.

China's rapid development has catapulted the country into the ranks of the world's largest economies, but it has also made it a top emitter of greenhouse gasses. The country has set ambitious goals for improving energy efficiency. China's plans to build more nuclear plants could help it avoid producing 8.4 gigatons of emissions annually that it might otherwise emit if growth continued without any mitigation. Still, Mckinsey's research finds there's room to do even more. Tapping emerging technologies, such as electric vehicles, new semiconductor-manufacturing equipment that's better at controlling fluorocarbon emissions, and the use of agricultural waste as a fuel source in cement kilns, could save an additional 6.7 gigatons.

The Pros and Cons of a Student Loan Program

21

Brainstorming

Brainstorm keywords and ideas related to the topic and address the given question. Then, make a speech and share your opinion.

Tuition

- **Scholarship**

  Do you think scholarship programs play a vital role in enabling students to continue their studies?

-

-

Reading

In an increasingly competitive job market, a college degree has **ceased to be optional**. This has led many students and their families **to borrow exorbitant sums** in order to finance an education, which they hope will be the stepping stone to a successful future. Once considered an investment, college has become more of **a financial burden** than a guarantee to a rewarding and well-paying career.

Given the harshness of the current economic climate, the volume of student loan debt has **soared to unprecedented highs**—more than $1 trillion in the US alone. As tuition prices continue on their upward rise, students are forced to borrow intimidating amounts of money only to face an unstable job market where approximately 300,000 American college graduates are forced to work minimum wage jobs.

In the US, the average borrower will graduate with around $40,000 in debt. Given the current state of the economy, many are finding it more challenging to repay their debts than expected. Although many student loans promise flexible payment schemes that allow recipients to lengthen the term or lower loan payments

dependent on income, this actually ends up costing them more in the long run. A shocking 6.8 million over-50s are still working off their student debt.

Student loans have **contributed to the rise of** an educated work force in countries around the globe. They help fund educations for many of those who might have been excluded for monetary reasons. Despite their innumerable benefits, these loans have also **compounded a rising youth debt problem**, and in some ways, have changed society forever. Student debt not only affects the credit of those who are burdened with it, but it also affects the decisions that they make. The pressure to keep up with the payments has caused many young entrepreneurs to give up on their dreams rather than risk becoming **a credit delinquent**.

Core Message

Talk about the core message of the article.

Chunk and Chew

Write the number of the meaningful chunk in the column next to its meaning. Then, by using each chunk, summarize something you have learned in the unit.

1 a financial burden	5 soared to unprecedented highs
2 contributed to the rise of	6 dependent on income
3 ceased to be optional	7 a credit delinquent
4 compounded a rising youth debt problem	8 to borrow exorbitant sums

to have become something necessary

to take out a loan for an extremely large amount of money

have helped to increase something

something that causes monetary discomfort

helped increase the worrying amount of loans held by young people

risen to an all-time high

people who default on loan payments

proportionate to the amount of money earned

1

2

3

4

5

6

7

8

Practice Discussing

1 Did you incur debt in the form of student loans while at university? How did you handle repaying that debt?

2 Are student loans the best way to help students meet the high cost of tuition, or should the government be taking steps to reduce the tuition cost for all students?

3 What are the pros and cons of scholarship programs for students?

4 All universities are not created equal. Do you think the government should impose a nationwide curriculum that all universities must use in order to standardize education across the country?

5 Do you think it would be reasonable for students to indefinitely defer payments on student loans when it becomes unbearable? Why or why not?

Debating

Statement

Government funding (i.e. tax revenues) should not be used to subsidize student tuition fees. The students are the ones who benefit from their education, and taxes should not be used to help individuals gain personal advantage.

Do you agree or disagree with this statement? Why or why not? Please be specific.

Opinion :

Reason :

Support 1.

Support 2.

Support 3.

Summarize the opposing ideas.

Any rebuttal?

STATISTICS

5th

Create an effective title for the following paragraph.

Private consumption in China totaled $890 billion in 2007, making the country the world's fifth-largest consumer market, behind the United States, Japan, the UK, and Germany (which China recently surpassed as the world's third-largest economy). But relative to China's population and level of economic development, its consumers punch far below their weight. The country's consumption-do-GDP ratio of 37% is only half that of the United States and about two-thirds the rates in Europe and Japan. Indeed, China has the lowest such ratio of any major world economy except Saudi Arabia, where oil exports constitute the bulk of economic output.

Eco-businesses: Best of Both Worlds!

22

Brainstorming

Brainstorm keywords and ideas related to the topic and address the given question. Then, make a speech and share your opinion.

Eco-business

- **Sustainability**

  What roles do individuals and corporations have in promoting sustainability? How do these roles differ?

Reading

Eco-business involves **stretching the concept of sustainability** to extend to both the environment and the businesses that engage in it. As environmentally friendly business practices rise in popularity, the efforts of their supporters **are not going unnoticed**. In this way, eco-business is inspiring individuals to follow big businesses' examples and strive to protect Earth's valuable resources.

Since 1990, when the Environmental Defense Fund first teamed up with McDonald's to eliminate Styrofoam sandwich containers, more and more non-government organizations (NGOs) have collaborated with Fortune 500 companies to try to reduce the environmental impact of their business choices. While critics **might be skeptical of the intentions of** these NGO/corporation partnerships, they are actually quite effective.

Even a small change in a global company's practices can affect a noticeable impact worldwide and, through the company's good example, **act as a catalyst** for positive social change. The benefits to companies are not limited to public relations—or even saving the environment. **Although it seems counter-**

intuitive, it is possible to achieve social responsibility while simultaneously maximizing profits. The retailer Marks & Spencer reported that employing sustainability measures saved them $110 million in 2011 alone.

Recently, some of the biggest names in business **have been jumping on the eco-business bandwagon**. Brands like General Electric and Wal-mart have been among those to implement environment friendly goals as a way of increasing profits. These plans have also enabled many companies to achieve greater command of supply chains and help the Earth, **all while gaining a leg up on their competition**.

Eco-business is the right choice for a variety of reasons. Along with helping our planet, companies are able to **further their own interests**. Due to its diverse benefits, the future of eco-business is looking bright. As companies work toward achieving environmental consciousness, future generations will undoubtedly reap the benefits for years to come.

Core Message

Talk about the core message of the article.

Chunk and Chew

The following sentences are from the article. Try to determine the meaning of each boldfaced phrase or chunk. Write a synonym or your own definition for each of the boldfaced phrases.

1 Eco-business involves **stretching the concept of sustainability** to extend to both the environment and the businesses that engages in it.

2 As environmentally friendly business practices rise in popularity, the efforts of their supporters **are not going unnoticed**.

3 While critics **might be skeptical of the intentions of** these NGO/corporation partnerships, they are actually quite effective.

4 Even a small change in a global company's practices can affect a noticeable impact worldwide and through the company's good example, **act as a catalyst** for positive social change."

5 **Although it seems counterintuitive**, it is possible to achieve social responsibility while simultaneously maximizing profits.

6 Recently, some of the biggest names in business **have been jumping on the eco-business bandwagon**.

7 These plans have also enabled many companies to achieve greater command of supply chains and help the Earth, **all while gaining a leg up on their competition**.

8 Along with helping our planet, companies are able to **further their own interests**.

Practice Discussing

1 What are some ways consumers can encourage big companies to lower the environmental impact of their business practices?

2 Is it feasible for the government to place stricter restrictions on companies to limit their environmental impact? Why or why not?

3 What needs to be done to increase awareness about environmental pollution?

4 Should we make the development of renewable energy sources an economic priority?

5 Give some examples of eco-businesses in your country. Are they successful?

Debating

Statement

Eco-business is an admirable idea, but getting big businesses to change is not as simple as it seems. For this reason, government intervention is necessary. If the government created stricter regulations, it would be possible to force all companies toward environmentally sound practices.

Do you agree or disagree with this statement? Why or why not? Please be specific.

Opinion :

Reason :

Support 1.

Support 2.

Support 3.

Summarize the opposing ideas.

Any rebuttal?

STATISTICS

8.2%

Create an effective title for the following paragraph.

A low-income man is 8.2 percentage points less likely to be married if his wages are below the median for his "reference group" – men who live in the same city, are of the same ethnicity, and have the same education, according to Tara Watson of Williams College and Sara McLanahan of Princeton. Men appear to perceive that marriage requires a certain level of income, a level determined by peers' wages, the researchers say. The effect doesn't apply to high-income men.

Electrifying Cars

23

Brainstorming

Brainstorm keywords and ideas related to the topic and address the given question. Then, make a speech and share your opinion.

Transportation

Electric Alternatives

What would be some of the biggest advantages in switching to electric cars?

Reading

Given the rising costs and **finite supply of fuel**, global warming effects from burning those fuels, and growing traffic congestion as well as air and noise pollution in our cities, can the private automobile continue as before with out **unbearable environmental consequences?** It is questions like these that have led Michelin, the French tire company, to hold the Challenge Bibendum, an annual global green vehicle conference with the declared aim of "rallying together towards sustainable road mobility". The 11th edition of the event, held in May in Berlin, brought together over 5,000 experts involved in road transport to discuss how to make vehicles and transport systems cleaner and more energy efficient. Indeed, the German capital was a fitting venue, for it was here that Karl Benz filed a patent for his motorwagen, the world's first automobile, back in 1886. But how do we move forward from here?

Michel Rollier, chief executive of Michelin group, notes that, at the first Challenge Bibendum, not many people were interested in these subjects. "Now, here in Berlin, there are 280 vehicles on display outside showing advances and innovations in intelligent mobility for the future." These included hybrid or full-electric cars, three-wheelers, motorbikes, and an intriguing array of electric-boosted bicycles. **Different strokes for different folks**.

While the Challenge Bibendum does acknowledge that buses are still the fastest and cheapest way to have an energy- efficient transport system, the main message is to demonstrate how we can still enjoy cars use while reducing CO2 emissions. We're not even talking about gas-electric hybrids but fully electric vehicles (EVs).

According to the event booklet on EVs, the main advantage of an electric over a gas motor is that is has 90 percent efficiency, meaning that 90 percent of electrical energy, is converted into mechanical energy, compared to only 35 percent for gas, since much of gas' chemical energy is lost as heat, etc. The cost of running EVs, kilometer by kilometer, should also be cheaper than gas cars. And finally, there is almost zero noise and air pollution from the vehicle itself. If the electricity used to charge the batteries comes from solar or hydro power, then the cycle is clean. Even if the juice comes from gas or coal, the energy used is still less than that used by a gas car.

However, the main drawback for EVs is not driving performance. It's **the lack of supporting infrastructure**. The C30 Electric, C-Zero, and Leaf all have ranges of about 150 km, beyond which the battery needs recharging. After over a century of fossil fuel addiction, the world has petrol pumps even in tiny villages, but even large cities lack electric car recharging stations. The challenge, then, is how recharging can be revolutionized to make it more convenient and simpler. Quick charge batteries and **battery swapping** are ideas that are being developed.

The world may have reached the limits of fossil fuels, what with current oil production already having **reached its peak**, and the possible climate and **ocean-rising disasters** from global warming. A massive switch to more energy-efficient public transport is an obvious answer. Since we still love driving our own cars, Michelin's Challenge Bibendum suggests some green solutions that may enable us to **have our cake and eat it too**.

Core Message

Talk about the core message of the article.

Chunk and Chew

The following sentences are from the article. Try to determine the meaning of each boldfaced phrase or chunk. Write a synonym or your own definition for each of the boldfaced phrases.

1 Given the rising costs and **finite supply of fuel,** global warming effects from burning those fuels, and growing traffic congestion as well as air and noise pollution in our cities, ...

2 Can the private automobile continue as before without **unbearable environmental consequences**?

3 These included hybrid or full-electric cars, three-wheelers, motorbikes, and an intriguing array of electric-boosted bicycles. **Different strokes for different folks**.

4 However, the main drawback for EVs is not driving performance. It's t**he lack of supporting infrastructure.**

5 Quick charge batteries and **battery swapping** are ideas that are being developed.

6 The world may have reached the limits of fossil fuels, what with current oil production already having **reached its peak**, ...

7 ... and the possible climate and **ocean-rising disasters** from global warming. A massive switch to more energy-efficient public transport is an obvious answer.

8 Since we still love driving our own cars, Michelin's Challenge Bibendum suggests some green solutions that may enable us to **have our cake and eat it too**.

In-depth Discussion Questions

1 Would you consider buying an electric car the next time you are ready to purchase a vehicle?
2 What would it take to convince you that buying an electric car was a good idea?
3 The technology to produce efficient, roadworthy electric cars has been around since 1996. What has prevented electric car technology from advancing faster?
4 Do you think it is possible that the internal combustion engines used today could be improved to be more efficient but are not because there is too much interest by the oil companies to sell gas and oil?
5 Do you think that electric powered transportation will completely replace gasoline power?

Debating

Statement

For now, electric cars are impractical. Until we completely run out of oil reserves on the planet, there will be no serious interest in changing the way we do things.

Do you agree or disagree with this statement? Why or why not? Please be specific.

Opinion :

Reason :

Support 1.

Support 2.

Support 3.

Summarize the opposing ideas.

Any rebuttal?

STATISTICS

10%↑

Create an effective title for the following paragraph.

A 10% increase in gasoline prices reduces traffic fatalities among U.S. adults aged 15 to 24 by 3.2% to 6.2%, according to Michael A. Morrisey of the University of Alabama at Birmingham and David C. Grabowski of Harvard Medical School. A 10% increase in beer taxes also cuts road deaths among this group but by a lower amount – an estimated 1.3%, the researchers say.

How About a Second Passport?

24

Brainstorming

Brainstorm keywords and ideas related to the topic and address the given question. Then, make a speech and share your opinion.

Citizenship

- Dual Citizenship

  Have you ever known anyone who had dual citizenship? Who was it, and why did they have it?

-

-

Reading

The Flannigans of Santa Rosa, California, have been American for several generations. They recently **jumped at the opportunity** to become new Irish citizens. The family had learned from an acquaintance that Irish passports were available to anyone with fully documented proof of an Irish grandparent. The Flannigans hired a private investigator to locate the Irish birth certificate of James Flannigan's grandmother, who came to America as a young child. Utilizing that document, first James, then his wife, and three of his four adult children put in applications to become Irish citizens. James's daughter, Caroline, said the passport has allowed her to work in both Italy and Austria since those countries, along with Ireland, are part of the European Union. Another sister has purchased property in Italy, and her own parents may well retire there.

All across the world, the children, grandchildren, and even great grandchildren of immigrant families are taking advantage of more open dual citizenship and right-of-return laws in order to obtain a second passport from the land of their ancestors. Some plan to return to their homeland while others seek to take full advantage of employment and living conditions within newly formed or expanded trade blocs in North America and the European Union. Nations often welcome those with **ancestral ties**, hoping to benefit from their skills and tax revenues, or, less often, for humanitarian reasons.

There are some immigration law experts who openly question whether countries should **give special consideration to** "co-ethnics," the majority of whom do not speak the language and have never lived in the country, while at the same time **tighten**ing residency and **citizenship requirements** for other migrants, who may have lived in the country for many years.

These regulations "may be acceptable if the country has a special obligation to protect an at-risk **co-ethnic minority**," stated Rainer Baubock, a recognized expert authority on European Union citizenship acquisition.

In other countries, the issue is not one of ethnicity, but of who has the ability to pay. The small Caribbean island country of Dominica, for example, sells citizenship for $75,000 in cash. Citizens of Dominica are not required to pay income tax on income made outside of the country and automatically become members of the British Commonwealth, which allows certain rights in Britain except the right to work.

There has been an **emerging trend** where countries strengthen ties with their diaspora by allowing them to keep their nationality whilst naturalizing in another nation. Countries such as India, Portugal, Italy, and the United States have modified regulations to allow dual citizenship.

Many other European nations have programs in place that selectively admit people with ancestral ties to that particular place. Certain EU states have started programs to block those with no ethnic connections from seeking citizenship in their country by requiring both history and language tests.

Of course, coming "home" for those who have not lived in the **country in question** can be quite a difficult experience, according to Emigrant Advice in Dublin, Ireland, a government-funded immigrant resource center. Most people will find a very different Ireland than the one they may have **pictured in their mind**.

Core Message

Talk about the core message of the article.

Chunk and Chew

The following sentences are from the article. Try to determine the meaning of each boldfaced phrase or chunk. Write a synonym or your own definition for each of the boldfaced phrases.

1 They recently **jumped at the opportunity** to become new Irish citizens.

2 Nations often welcome those with **ancestral ties**, hoping to benefit from their skills and tax revenues, or, less often, for humanitarian reasons.

3 There are some immigration law experts who openly question whether countries should **give special consideration** to "co-ethics."

4 ... the majority of whom do not speak the language and have never lived in the country, while at the same time **tighten**ing residency and **citizenship requirements** for other migrants, who may have lived in the country for many years.

5 These regulations "may be acceptable if the country has a special obligation to protect an at-risk **co-ethnic minority**," stated Rainer Baubock.

6 There has been an **emerging trend** where countries strengthen ties with their diaspora by allowing them to keep their nationality whilst naturalizing in another nation.

7 Of course, coming "home" for those who have not lived in the **country in question** can be quite a difficult experience.

8 Most people will find a very different Ireland than the one they may have **pictured in their mind**.

Practice Discussing

1 What are some reasons people may want dual citizenship?
2 Which country do you think has an exemplary dual citizenship policy?
3 What are some of the advantages and disadvantages of having dual citizenship?
4 Does dual citizenship represent a kind of freedom of association?
5 Is patriotism an important issue for dual citizenship?

Debating

Statement

Allowing children or grandchildren of natives to apply for citizenship is nothing more than a tax grab for the country's government.

Do you agree or disagree with this statement? Why or why not? Please be specific.

Opinion :

Reason :

Support 1.

Support 2.

Support 3.

Summarize the opposing ideas.

Any rebuttal?

STATISTICS

5

WORDS

Create an effective title for the following paragraph.

The five words most commonly used by extroverted bloggers are "bar," "other," "drinks," "restaurant," and "dancing," according to a study of the personalities and writings of 700 bloggers by Tal Yarkoni, a psychology and neuroscience postdoctoral fellow at the University of Colorado. By examining language use and personality types, Yarkoni also found that the top five words used by conscientious people are "completed," "adventure," "stupid," "boring," and "adventures."

Memo

Answer Key

Dynamic Discussion

Answer Key

Topic 01.

Chunk and Chew
5, 3, 4, 1, 6, 8, 7, 2

Statistics
Waitresses Who Stand Closer Get Better Tips

Topic 02.

Chunk and Chew
8, 6, 5, 3, 7, 4, 1, 2

Statistics
Diaper Sales Hint That Parents Are Economizing

Topic 03.

Chunk and Chew
4, 2, 3, 1, 5, 8, 7, 6

Statistics
Delaying Having Children Boosts Women's Pay

Topic 04.

Statistics
Rich Parents Withhold Asset Details from Kids

Topic 05.

Statistics
The 24/7 Employee

Topic 06.

Statistics
People Born in Economic Booms Live Longer

Topic 07.

Chunk and Chew
2, 1, 8, 4, 3, 5, 7, 6

Statistics
Declines in Retirement Savings Continue

Topic 08.

Chunk and Chew
3, 8, 4, 5, 1, 2, 7, 6

Statistics
Reseeding R&D

Topic 09.

Chunk and Chew
5, 4, 2, 8, 1, 7, 3, 6

Statistics
Tiny Plastic Debris Is Widespread in Mediterranean

Topic 10.

Statistics
More Dads Become Primary Caregivers

Topic 11.

Statistics
Smoke? No Thanks, I'm Too Busy Texting

Topic 12.

Statistics
Why the Youngs and Zanes Are Impatient to Buy

Topic 13.

Chunk and Chew

1, 3, 5, 4, 2, 8, 6, 7

Statistics

In Russia, Bribes Make the World Go Round

Topic 14.

Chunk and Chew

6, 8, 4, 3, 7, 2, 1, 5

Statistics

Multitasking 101

Topic 15.

Chunk and Chew

7, 6, 1, 3, 4, 5, 2, 8

Statistics

Credit Card Agreements Too Complicated for Most

Topic 16.

Statistics

Ex-Student Puts His Bachelor's Degree Up for Auction

Topic 17.

Statistics

Starbucks' Calorie Postings Lead to Less Calorie Consumption

Topic 18.

Statistics

Broken Supply Chains, Broken Trust

Topic 19.

Chunk and Chew

8, 7, 5, 1, 6, 4, 3, 2

Statistics

Clean Tech Won't Provide a Lot of Jobs

Topic 20.

Chunk and Chew

7, 8, 6, 1, 2, 3, 5, 4

Statistics

China's Green Opportunity

Topic 21.

Chunk and Chew

3, 8, 2, 1, 4, 5, 7, 6

Statistics

China: Learning to Spend

Topic 22.

Statistics

Men Judge Their Marriageability By Peers' Income

Topic 23.

Statistics

Gas Prices Limit Young Drivers' Road Deaths

Topic 24.

Statistics

Extroverted Bloggers Have Partying on the Mind